BE
CONFIDENT

BE

CONFIDENT

LIVE BY FAITH, NOT BY SIGHT

NT COMMENTARY

HEBREWS

Warren W. Wiersbe

transforming lives together

BE CONFIDENT
Published by David C. Cook
4050 Lee Vance View
Colorado Springs, CO 80918 U.S.A.

David C. Cook Distribution Canada
55 Woodslee Avenue, Paris, Ontario, Canada N3L 3E5

David C. Cook U.K., Kingsway Communications
Eastbourne, East Sussex BN23 6NT, England

David C. Cook and the graphic circle C logo
are registered trademarks of Cook Communications Ministries.

Unless otherwise noted, all Scripture quotations are taken from the King James Version of
the Bible. (Public Domain.) Scripture quotations marked NASB are taken from the *New
American Standard Bible*, © Copyright 1960, 1995 by The Lockman Foundation. Used by
permission; NIV are taken from the *Holy Bible, New International Version*®. *NIV*®. Copyright
© 1973, 1978, 1984 by International Bible Society. Used by permission of Zondervan. All
rights reserved; TLB are taken from *The Living Bible,* © 1971, Tyndale House Publishers,
Wheaton, IL 60189. Used by permission; and AB are taken from *The Amplified Bible*. Copyright © 1954, 1958, 1962, 1964, 1965, 1987 by The Lockman Foundation. Used by
permission. All italics in Scripture have been added by the author for emphasis.

LCCN 2008937430
ISBN 978-1-4347-6735-6
eISBN 978-1-4347-0313-2

First edition of *Be Confident* by Warren W. Wiersbe published by Victor Books®
in 1982 © Warren W. Wiersbe, ISBN 978-0-89693-728-4

The Team: Karen Lee-Thorp, Amy Kiechlin, Jack Campbell, and Susan Vannaman
Series Cover Design: John Hamilton Design
Cover Photo: Veer Inc.

Printed in the United States of America
Second Edition 2009

5 6 7 8 9 10 11 12

101310

*This book in the "BE" series is
dedicated to my good friend JIM ADAIR
whose editorial skill and constant
encouragement have shepherded me
through many days of study and writing.
Thanks, Jim!*

CONTENTS

THE BIG IDEA

An Introduction to *Be Confident*
by Ken Baugh

Dr. Viktor Frankl was an Austrian psychiatrist who lived as a prisoner in Auschwitz and other concentration camps during World War II. Dr. Frankl experienced unimaginable horror during his years of captivity, yet during that time he was able to discern the reasons why some people survived the camps while others did not. In his book *Man's Search for Meaning*, Dr. Frankl writes about how hope was the key factor to a prisoner's ability to survive. He says,

> For the prisoner who had lost faith in the future, his future was doomed. With his loss of belief in the future, he also lost his spiritual hold; he let himself decline and become subject to mental and physical decay.... The only chance people had of making it in the camps was their ability to focus on some future goal, it had nothing to do with who was the healthiest or strongest, but who had someone waiting back home for them or who had some vocational goal they dreamed of realizing one day. (Beacon, 2000, p. 82)

It surprises me that hope helped people survive the concentration camps. One would think it would be something more tangible like good health, food, warm clothing, and shelter; but, as Dr. Frankl discovered, it was the power of hope.

At times, life is dark and ominous. I cannot think of a season in my life that could ever equal that of Dr. Frankl's, but I have had my share of difficulties and no doubt so have you. Yet one thing that always serves me well during a difficult season of life is my confidence in God's character— that He can be trusted even during my darkest days. In fact, the Big Idea that runs throughout the book of Hebrews is simply this: You can trust God. And throughout the book, especially in chapters 11—12, we discover men and women of faith who have done just that, trusted God despite difficult circumstances.

We are reminded of the confidence of Abraham, Isaac, and Jacob as our forefathers in the faith. We read of Joseph and how he trusted God even after being unjustly accused and thrown into prison. We are reminded of Moses and his willingness to leave the riches of Egypt because of his confidence in God. And there are so many others—Rahab, Gideon, Barak, Jephthah, David, Samuel. All these people knew that they could trust God, and we remember them as great men and women of faith.

But if you're like me, as you read the stories of these people, it's tempting to think that they're different from you and me, that they had some type of supernatural gift of faith that we do not have that enabled them to trust God so completely. However, I don't think that's the case at all. I think they were just as normal as we are, and I believe that their level of faith is available to every follower of Christ. That's right: You, too, can become a great man or woman of faith if you remember the following three principles.

The first principle of great faith is *I must remember that God is with me.* This is a truth that we all know but need to be reminded of time and again. David says, "Even when walking through the dark valley of death I will not be afraid, for you are close beside me, guarding, guiding all the way" (Ps. 23:4 TLB). Jesus promised us that He would never leave us. He is always watching over us, and He knows exactly what's going on in our lives. The apostle Paul assures us that God will never give us more than we can bear (1 Cor. 10:13). He is constantly monitoring everything in our lives. We may not like the fact that God allows bad things to happen to us, but we can be confident that He is using even those things for our good and His glory. "The works of his hands are faithful and just; all his precepts are trustworthy" (Ps. 111:7 NIV).

The second principle of great faith is *I must remember the honor and rewards that await me in heaven*. The writer of Hebrews reminds us that it was the certainty of heaven that helped Jesus endure the cross. "Let us fix our eyes on Jesus, the author and perfecter of our faith, who for *the joy set before him* endured the cross, scorning its shame, and sat down at the right hand of the throne of God" (12:2 NIV). Jesus kept one eye on the reality of heaven, one eye on eternity, and it enabled Him to endure the pain, humiliation, and rejection He experienced on the cross. The same will be true of us if, during the difficult seasons in life, we remember that heaven is sure and that we will each be rewarded for our faithfulness to God during this life. Paul says, "These troubles and sufferings of ours are, after all, quite small and won't last very long. Yet this short time of distress will result in God's richest blessing upon us forever and ever!" (2 Cor. 4:17 TLB).

The third principle of great faith is *I must remember that God will guide me when I am confused*. Confusion is a close companion during difficult times, but if I look at my life and situation through the vantage point of God's Word, the confusion clears and I can better see God's purpose.

When NASA launches a rocket, their job is not over after the launch. Instead, NASA constantly monitors the rocket's progress, and the rocket continually receives instructions from ground control to keep it on the right heading. A rocket can reach its destination only if it maintains constant contact with ground control, and the same is true for each of us. The Bible says, "Trust God from the bottom of your heart; don't try to figure out everything on your own. Listen for God's voice in everything you do, every-where you go; he's the one who will keep you on track" (Prov. 3:5–6 TLB).

Every believer can develop great faith if we remember these three prin-ciples. I have no doubt that as you study the book of Hebrews along with Dr. Wiersbe's commentary, you will be strengthened in your faith and encouraged in your walk with God.

***

Dr. Wiersbe's commentaries have been a source of guidance and strength to me over the many years that I have been a pastor. His unique style is not overly academic, but theologically sound. He explains the deep truths of Scripture in a way that everyone can understand and apply. Whether you're a Bible scholar or a brand-new believer in Christ, you will benefit, as I have, from Warren's insights. With your Bible in one hand and Dr. Wiersbe's commentary in the other, you will be able to accurately unpack the deep truths of God's Word and learn how to apply them to your life.

Drink deeply, my friend, of the truths of God's Word, for in them you will find Jesus Christ, and there is freedom, peace, assurance, and joy.

—Ken Baugh
Pastor of Coast Hills Community Church
Aliso Viejo, California

A WORD FROM THE AUTHOR

The epistle to the Hebrews is a book we need today. It was written at a time when the ages were colliding and when everything in society seemed to be shaken. It was written to Christians who were wondering what was going on and what they could do about it. The stability of the old was passing away, and their faith was wavering.

One of the major messages of Hebrews is *Be Confident*! God is shaking things so that you may learn to live by faith and not by sight. He wants you to build your life on the permanence of the eternal and not on the instability of the temporal.

This is the message I have tried to bring out in this brief exposition. I have had to deal only briefly with some truths, and totally ignore others, so that this message might come across. It is impossible in a book this size to cover everything in so profound an epistle as Hebrews.

You may not agree with all my interpretations and applications. But if you are a Christian I am sure you will agree that our ever-living High Priest in heaven is able to see us through these difficult and demanding days. "The just shall live by faith!"

Look to Jesus Christ and—*Be Confident*!

—Warren W. Wiersbe

A Suggested Outline of the Book of Hebrews

Theme: Press on to maturity
Key verse: Hebrews 6:1

I. A Superior Person—Christ (Hebrews 1—6)
    A. Better than the prophets (Hebrews 1:1–3)
    B. Better than the angels (Hebrews 1:4—2:18)
        (Exhortation: drifting from the Word: 2:1–4)
    C. Better than Moses (Hebrews 3:1—4:13)
        (Exhortation: doubting the Word: 3:7—4:13)
    D. Better than Aaron (Hebrews 4:14—6:20)
        (Exhortation: dullness toward the Word: 5:11—6:20)

II. A Superior Priesthood—Melchizedek (Hebrews 7—10)
    A. A superior order (Hebrews 7)
    B. A superior covenant (Hebrews 8)
    C. A superior sanctuary (Hebrews 9)
    D. A superior sacrifice (Hebrews 10)
        (Exhortation: despising the Word: 10:26–39)

III. A Superior Principle—Faith (Hebrews 11—13)
    A. The great examples of faith (Hebrews 11)
    B. The endurance of faith—chastening (Hebrews 12)
        (Exhortation: defying the Word: 12:14–29)
    C. Closing: practical exhortations (Hebrews 13)

Chapter One

Is Anybody Listening?

(Hebrews 1:1–3)

A man from Leeds, England, visited his doctor to have his hearing checked. The doctor removed the man's hearing aid, and the patient's hearing immediately improved! He had been wearing the device *in the wrong ear* for over twenty years!

I once asked a pastor friend, "Do you have a deaf ministry in your church?" He replied, "There are times when I think the whole church needs a deaf ministry—they just don't seem to hear me."

There is a difference between *listening* and really *hearing*. Jesus often cried, "He who has ears to hear, let him hear!" This statement suggests that it takes more than physical ears to hear the voice of God. It also requires a receptive heart. "To day if ye will hear his voice, harden not your hearts" (Heb. 3:7–8).

Many people have avoided the epistle to the Hebrews and, consequently, have robbed themselves of practical spiritual help. Some have avoided this book because they are afraid of it. The "warnings" in Hebrews have made them uneasy. Others have avoided this book because they think it is "too difficult" for the average Bible student. To be sure, there are some profound truths in Hebrews, and no preacher or teacher would dare to claim that he knows them all! But the general message of the book is clear and there is no reason why you and I should not understand and profit from it.

Perhaps the best way to begin our study is to notice five characteristics of the epistle to the Hebrews.

1. It Is a Book of Evaluation

The word *better* is used thirteen times in this book as the writer shows the superiority of Jesus Christ and His salvation over the Hebrew system of religion. Christ is "better than the angels" (Heb. 1:4). He brought in "a better hope" (Heb. 7:19) because He is the mediator of "a better covenant, which was established upon better promises" (Heb. 8:6).

Another word that is repeated in this book is *perfect;* in the original Greek it is used fourteen times. It means "a perfect standing before God." This perfection could never be accomplished by the Levitical priesthood (Heb. 7:11) or by the law (Heb. 7:19), nor could the blood of animal sacrifices achieve it (Heb. 10:1). Jesus Christ gave Himself as one offering for sin, and by this He has "perfected for ever them that are sanctified" (Heb. 10:14).

So the writer was contrasting the Old Testament system of law with the New Testament ministry of grace. He was making it clear that the Jewish religious system was temporary and that it could not bring in the eternal "better things" that are found in Jesus Christ.

Eternal is a third word that is important to the message of Hebrews. Christ is the "author of eternal salvation" (Heb. 5:9). Through His death, He "obtained eternal redemption" (Heb. 9:12), and He shares with believers "the promise of eternal inheritance" (Heb. 9:15). His throne is forever (Heb. 1:8) and He is a priest forever (Heb. 5:6; 6:20; 7:17, 21). "Jesus Christ, the same yesterday, and to day, and for ever" (Heb. 13:8).

When you combine these three important words, you discover that Jesus Christ and the Christian life He gives us are *better* because these blessings are *eternal* and they give us a *perfect* standing before God. The religious system under the Mosaic law was imperfect because it could not accomplish a once-for-all redemption that was eternal.

But why did the writer ask his readers to evaluate their faith and what Jesus Christ had to offer them? Because they were going through difficult times and were being tempted to go back to the Jewish religion. The temple was still standing when this book was written, and all the priestly ceremonies were still being carried on daily. How easy it would have been for these Jewish believers to escape persecution by going back into the old Mosaic system that they had known before.

These people were second-generation believers, having been won to Christ by those who had known Jesus Christ during His ministry on earth (Heb. 2:3). They were true believers (Heb. 3:1) and not mere professors. They had been persecuted because of their faith (Heb. 10:32–34; 12:4; 13:13–14), and yet they had faithfully ministered to the needs of others who had suffered (Heb. 6:10). But they were being seduced by teachers of false doctrine (Heb. 13:9), and they were in danger of forgetting the true Word that their first leaders, now dead, had taught them (Heb. 13:7).

The tragic thing about these believers is that they were at a standstill spiritually and in danger of going backward (Heb. 5:12ff.). Some of them had even forsaken the regular worship services (Heb. 10:25) and were not making spiritual progress (Heb. 6:1). In the Christian life, if you do not go forward, you go backward; there is no permanent standing still.

"How can you go back into your former religion?" the writer asked them. "Just take time to evaluate what you have in Jesus Christ. He is better than anything you ever had under the law."

The book of Hebrews exalts the person and the work of Jesus Christ, the Son of God. When you realize all that you have in and through Him, you have no desire for anyone else or anything else!

2. It Is a Book of Exhortation

The writer called this epistle "the word of exhortation" (Heb. 13:22). The Greek word translated "exhortation" simply means "encouragement." It is translated "comfort" in Romans 15:4, and "consolation" in 2 Corinthians 1:5–7; 7:7. This word is related to the Greek word translated "Comforter" in John 14:16, referring to the Holy Spirit. The epistle to the Hebrews was not written to frighten people, but to encourage people. We are commanded to "encourage one another daily" (Heb. 3:13 NIV). It reminds us that we have "strong encouragement" in Jesus Christ (Heb. 6:18 NASB).

At this point we must answer the usual question: "But what about those five terrible warnings found in Hebrews?"

To begin with, these five passages are not really "warnings." Three basic words are translated "warn" in the New Testament, and the only one used in Hebrews is translated "admonished" in Hebrews 8:5 (where it refers to Moses) and "spake" in Hebrews 12:25. Only in Hebrews 11:7 is it translated "warned," where it refers to Noah "being warned of God." I think that the best description of the five so-called warning passages is the one given in Hebrews 13:22—"exhortation" (KJV), or "encouragement" (AB). This does not minimize the seriousness of these five sections of the book, but it does help us grasp their purpose: to encourage us to trust God and heed His Word.

The epistle to the Hebrews opens with an important declaration: "God … has spoken to us in His Son" (Heb. 1:1–2 NASB). Near the close of the book, the writer states, "See to it that you do not refuse Him who is speaking" (Heb. 12:25 NASB). In other words, the theme of Hebrews seems to be "God has spoken; we have His Word. What are we doing about it?"

With this truth in mind, we can now better understand the significance of those five "problem passages" in Hebrews. Each of these passages encourages us to heed God's Word ("God … has spoken") by pointing out the sad spiritual consequences that result if we do not. Let me list these passages for you and explain their sequence in the book of Hebrews. I think you will see how they all hang together and present one message: *Heed God's Word.*

> *Drifting* from the Word—2:1–4 (neglect)
> *Doubting* the Word—3:7—4:13 (hard heart)
> *Dullness* toward the Word—5:11—6:20 (sluggishness)
> *Despising* the Word—10:26–39 (willfulness)
> *Defying* the Word—12:14–29 (refusing to hear)

If we do not listen to God's Word and really *hear* it, we will start to *drift*. Neglect always leads to drifting, in things material and physical as well as spiritual. As we drift from the Word, we start to *doubt* the Word, because *faith* comes by hearing the Word of God (Rom. 10:17). We start to get hard hearts, and this leads to spiritual sluggishness, which produces *dullness* toward the Word. We become "dull of hearing"—lazy listeners! This leads to a *despiteful* attitude toward the Word to the extent that we willfully *disobey* God, and this gradually develops into a *defiant* attitude— we almost "dare" God to do anything!

Now what does God do while this spiritual regression is going on? He keeps speaking to us, encouraging us to get back to the Word. If we fail to listen and obey, then He begins to chasten us. This chastening process is the theme of Hebrews 12, the climactic chapter in the epistle. "The Lord shall judge *his people*" (Heb. 10:30). God does not allow His children to become "spoiled brats" by permitting them to willfully defy His Word. He always chastens in love.

These five exhortations are addressed to people who are truly born again. Their purpose is to get the readers to pay close attention to God's Word. While there is some stern language in some of these passages, it is my understanding that none of these exhortations "threatens" the reader by suggesting that he may "lose his salvation." If he persists in defying God's Word, he may lose *his life* ("Shall we not much rather be in subjection unto the Father of spirits, and live?" [Heb. 12:9]). The inference is that if we do not submit, we might die. "There is a sin unto death" (1 John 5:16). But if the epistle to the Hebrews teaches anything, it teaches the assurance of eternal life in a living High Priest who can never die (Heb. 7:22–28).

Some students try to explain away the "problem" of "losing your salvation" or "apostasy" by claiming that the readers were not truly born again, but were only "professors" of Christian faith. However, the way the writer addresses them would eliminate that approach; for he called them "holy brethren, partakers of the heavenly calling" (Heb. 3:1). He told them that they had a High Priest in heaven (Heb. 4:14), which he would not have written if they were lost. They had been "made partakers of the Holy Ghost" (Heb. 6:4). The admonitions in Hebrews 10:19–25 would be meaningless if addressed to unsaved people.

The epistle to the Hebrews is a book of evaluation, proving that Jesus Christ is better than anything the law of Moses has to offer. The epistle is also a book of exhortation, urging its readers to hear and heed the Word of God, lest they regress spiritually and experience the chastening hand of God.

3. IT IS A BOOK OF EXAMINATION

As you study this book, you will find yourself asking: "What am I *really* trusting? Am I trusting the Word of God, or am I trusting the things of this world that are shaking and ready to fall away?"

This letter was written to believers at a strategic time in history. The temple was still standing and the sacrifices were still being offered. But in a few years, both the city and the temple would be destroyed. The Jewish nation would be scattered, and this would include Jewish believers in Jesus Christ. The ages were colliding! God was "shaking" the order of things (Heb. 12:25–29). He wanted His people to have their feet on the solid foundation of faith; He did not want them to trust in things that would vanish.

I believe that the church today is living in similar circumstances. Everything around us is shaking and changing. People are discovering that they have been depending on the "scaffolding" and not on the solid foundation. Even God's people have gotten so caught up in this world's system that their confidence is not in the Lord, but in money, buildings, programs, and other passing material things. As God continues to "shake" society, the scaffolding will fall away, and God's people will discover that their only confidence must be in the Word of God.

God wants our hearts to be "established with grace" (Heb. 13:9). That word *established* is used, in one form or another, eight times in Hebrews. It means "to be solidly grounded, to stand firm on your feet." It carries the idea of strength, reliability, confirmation, permanence. This, I think, is the key message of Hebrews: "You can be secure while everything around you is falling apart!" We have a "kingdom which cannot be moved" (Heb. 12:28). God's Word is steadfast (Heb. 2:2) and so is the hope we have in Him (Heb. 6:19).

Of course, there is no security for a person who has never trusted Jesus Christ as his own Savior from sin. Nor is there security to those who have made a "lip profession" but whose lives do not give evidence of true salvation (Matt. 7:21–27; Titus 1:16). Christ saves "to the uttermost" (i.e., "eternally") only those who have come to God through faith in Him (Heb. 7:25).

I like to tell congregations the story about the conductor who got on the train, began to take tickets, and told the first passenger whose ticket he took, "Sir, you're on the wrong train." When he looked at the next ticket, he told that passenger the same thing.

"But the brakeman told me to get on this train," the passenger protested.

"I'll double-check," said the conductor. He did and discovered that *he* was on the wrong train!

I fear there are many people who have a false faith, who have not really heard and heeded God's Word. Sometimes they are so busy telling everybody else what to do that they fail to examine their own situations. The epistle to the Hebrews is a book of examination: it helps you discover where your faith really is.

4. It Is a Book of Expectation

The focus in this book is on the future. The writer informs us that he is speaking about "the world to come" (Heb. 2:5), a time when believers will reign with Christ. Jesus Christ is "heir of all things" (Heb. 1:2) and we share the "promise of eternal inheritance" (Heb. 9:15). Like the patriarchs lauded in Hebrews 11, we are looking for that future city of God (Heb. 11:10–16, 26).

Like these great men and women of faith, we today should be "strangers and pilgrims on the earth" (Heb. 11:13). This is one reason why God is shaking everything around us. *He wants us to turn loose from the things of this world and stop depending on them.* He wants us to center our attention on the world to come. This does *not* mean that we become so heavenly minded that we're no earthly good. Rather it means that we "hang loose" as far as this world is concerned, and start living for the eternal values of the world to come.

Abraham and Lot, his nephew, illustrate these two different attitudes (Gen. 13—14). Abraham was a wealthy man who could have lived in an expensive house in any location that he chose. But he was first of all God's servant, a pilgrim and a stranger, and this meant living in tents. Lot chose to abandon the pilgrim life and move into the evil city of Sodom. Which of these two men had true security? It would appear that Lot was safer in the city than Abraham was in his tents on the plain. But Lot became a prisoner of war! And Abraham had to rescue him.

Instead of heeding God's warning, Lot went back into the city, and when God destroyed Sodom and Gomorrah, Lot lost everything (Gen. 19). Lot was a saved man (2 Peter 2:7), but he trusted in the things of this world instead of trusting the Word of God. Lot forfeited the permanent because he depended on and lived for the immediate.

Martyred missionary Jim Elliot said it best: "He is no fool who gives what he cannot keep to gain what he cannot lose."

You and I as God's children have been promised a future reward. As with Abraham and Moses of old, the decisions we make today will determine the rewards tomorrow. More than this, our decisions should be motivated by the expectation of receiving rewards. Abraham obeyed God *because* "he looked for a city" (Heb. 11:10). Moses forsook the treasures and the pleasures of Egypt *because* "he had respect unto the recompense of the reward" (Heb. 11:26). These great men and women (Heb. 11:31, 35) of faith "lived in the future tense" and thus were able to overcome the temptations of the world and the flesh.

In fact, it was this same attitude of faith that carried our Lord Jesus Christ through the agony of the cross: "Jesus ... for the joy that was set before him endured the cross, despising the shame" (Heb. 12:2). The emphasis in the epistle to the Hebrews is "Don't live for what the world will promise you today! Live for what God has promised you in the future! Be a stranger and a pilgrim on this earth! Walk by faith, not by sight!"

This letter is not a diet for "spiritual babes" who want to be spoon-fed and coddled (Heb. 5:11–14). In this letter you will find "strong meat" that demands some "spiritual molars" for chewing and enjoying. The emphasis in Hebrews is not on what Christ did on the earth (the "milk"), but what

He is now doing in heaven (the "meat" of the Word). He is the Great High Priest who *enables us* by giving us grace (Heb. 4:14–16). He is also the Great Shepherd of the sheep who *equips us* to do His will (Heb. 13:20–21). He is working *in us* to accomplish His purposes. What a thrill it is for us to be a part of such a marvelous ministry!

Dr. A. W. Tozer used to remind us, "Every man must choose his world." True believers have "tasted the good word of God, and the powers of the world [age] to come" (Heb. 6:5); this should mean we have no interest in or appetite for the present sinful world system. Abraham chose the right world and became the father of the faithful. Lot chose the wrong world and became the father of the enemies of God's people (Gen. 19:30–38). Abraham became the friend of God (2 Chron. 20:7), but Lot became the friend of the world—and lost everything. Lot was "saved; yet so as by fire" (1 Cor. 3:15) and lost his reward.

5. It Is a Book of Exaltation

The epistle to the Hebrews exalts the person and the work of our Lord Jesus Christ. The first three verses set this high and holy theme, which is maintained throughout the entire book. Their immediate purpose is to prove that Jesus Christ is superior to the prophets, men who were held in the highest esteem by the Jewish people.

In His person, Christ is superior to the prophets. To begin with, He is the very Son of God and not merely a man called by God. The author makes it clear that Jesus Christ is God (Heb. 1:3), for his description could never be applied to mortal man. "Brightness of his glory" refers to the shekinah glory of God that dwelt in the tabernacle and temple. (See Ex. 40:34–38 and 1 Kings 8:10. The word *Shekinah* is a transliteration of a Hebrew word that means "to dwell.") Christ is to the Father what the rays of the sun are to the sun. He is the radiance of God's glory. As it is impossible to separate the rays from the sun, it is also impossible to separate Christ's glory from the nature of God.

"Express image" (Heb. 1:3) carries the idea of "the exact imprint." Our English word *character* comes from the Greek word translated "image." Literally, Jesus Christ is "the exact representation of the very substance of God" (see Col. 2:9). Only Jesus could honestly say, "He that hath seen me hath seen the Father" (John 14:9). When you see Christ, you see the glory of God (John 1:14).

In His work, Christ is also superior to the prophets. To begin with, He is the *Creator* of the universe, for by Him, God "made the worlds" (Heb. 1:2). Not only did Christ create all things by His Word (John 1:1–5), but He also upholds all things by that same powerful Word (Heb. 1:3). "And he is before all things, and by him all things consist [hold together]" (Col. 1:17).

The word *upholding* (Heb. 1:3) does not mean "holding up," as though the universe is a burden on the back of Jesus. It means "holding and carrying from one place to another." He is the God of creation and the God of providence who guides this universe to its divinely ordained destiny.

He is also the superior *Prophet* who declares God's Word. The contrast between Christ the Prophet and the other prophets is easy to see:

Christ	*The Prophets*
God the Son	Men called by God
One Son	Many prophets
A final and complete message	A fragmentary and incomplete message

Of course, both the Old Testament and the gospel revelation came from God, but Jesus Christ was God's "last word" as far as revelation is concerned. Christ is the source, center, and end of everything that God has to say.

But Jesus Christ has a ministry as *Priest,* and this reveals His greatness. By Himself He "purged our sins" (Heb. 1:3). This aspect of His ministry will be explained in detail in Hebrews 7—10.

Finally, Jesus Christ reigns as *King* (Heb. 1:3). He has sat down, for His work is finished, and He has sat down "on the right hand of the Majesty on high," the place of honor. This proves that He is equal with God the Father, for no mere created being could ever sit at God's right hand.

Creator, Prophet, Priest, and King—Jesus Christ is superior to all of the prophets and servants of God who have ever appeared on the sacred pages of the Scriptures. It is no wonder that the Father said, at the hour of Christ's transfiguration, "This is my beloved Son, in whom I am well pleased; hear ye him" (Matt. 17:5). Two of the greatest prophets were there with Jesus—Moses and Elijah, but Christ is superior to them.

As we study Hebrews together, we must keep in mind that our purpose is not to get lost in curious doctrinal details. Nor is our purpose to attack or defend some pet doctrine. Our purpose is to hear God speak in Jesus Christ, and to heed that Word. We want to echo the prayer of the Greeks: "Sir, we would see Jesus" (John 12:21). If our purpose is to know Christ better and exalt Him more, then whatever differences we may have in our understanding of the book will be forgotten in our worship of Him.

QUESTIONS FOR PERSONAL REFLECTION
OR GROUP DISCUSSION

1. What is the difference between hearing and really listening?

2. In what ways do you agree or disagree with this statement: "In the Christian life, if you do not go forward, you go backward; there is no permanent standing still"?

3. Wiersbe says, "God does not allow His children to become 'spoiled brats.'" What are some traits of a "spoiled brat" Christian?

4. Name some things that we tend to trust in today rather than trusting in God.

5. Wiersbe says that the book of Hebrews is a book of examination. It helps us discover where our faith is. What sometimes keeps us from examining our lives?

6. Abraham understood a sense of values and delayed gratification. Lot on the other hand lived for the immediate. List examples of Abrahams and Lots in today's world.

7. Hebrews sets out to prove Christ is not merely a man. What difference would it make in your life if you discovered that Christ was indeed merely a good man or a prophet?

8. Read Genesis 1:26, John 1:1–14, and Colossians 1:13–17. Then explain Christ's role before the Incarnation.

9. Tozer is quoted as saying, "Every man must choose his world." What makes it difficult at times to choose the kingdom of heaven over the kingdom of earth?

Chapter Two

GREATER THAN ANGELS

(Hebrews 1:4—2:18)

Angels were most important in the Jewish religion, primarily because thousands of angels assisted in the giving of the law at Mount Sinai. This fact is stated in Deuteronomy 33:2 (where "saints" in KJV means "holy ones" or "angels"); Psalm 68:17; Acts 7:53; and Galatians 3:19. Since the theme of Hebrews is the superiority of Christ and His salvation to the law of Moses, the writer would have to deal with the important subject of angels.

This long section on angels is divided into three parts. First, there is an *affirmation* (Heb. 1:4–14) of the superiority of Christ to the angels. The proof presented consists of seven quotations from the Old Testament. Second, there is an *exhortation* (Heb. 2:1–4) that the readers (and this includes us) pay earnest heed to the Word God has given through His Son. Finally, there is an *explanation* (Heb. 2:5–18) as to how Christ, with a human body, could still be superior to angels, who are spirits.

1. AFFIRMATION: CHRIST IS SUPERIOR TO THE ANGELS (1:4–14)

This section is comprised of seven quotations from the Old Testament, all of which prove the superiority of Christ to the angels. Scholars tell us that the writer quoted from the Greek version of the Hebrew Old Testament, known as the Septuagint. (The word *Septuagint* is a Greek word that means "seventy." Tradition claims that seventy men translated the Hebrew Old Testament into the Greek. The abbreviation for Septuagint is LXX, Roman numerals for seventy.) However, the same Holy Spirit who inspired the Scriptures has the right to quote and restate the truth as He sees fit.

Let us note the affirmations that are made about our Lord Jesus Christ, and the quotations that are cited to support them.

He is the Son (vv. 4–5). The "more excellent name" that Jesus possesses is "Son." While the angels *collectively* may be termed "the sons of God" (Job 1:6), no angel would be given this title *individually*. It belongs uniquely to our Lord Jesus Christ. The first quotation is from Psalm 2:7: "Thou art my Son; this day have I begotten thee." Paul pinpointed the time of this "begetting": the resurrection of Jesus Christ (Acts 13:33). From eternity, Jesus Christ was God the Son. He humbled Himself and became Man (see Phil. 2:5–6). In His resurrection, however, He glorified that humanity received from the Father and received back the eternal glory He had veiled (John 17:1, 5). The resurrection declares, "Jesus is God's Son!" (see Rom. 1:4).

The second quotation is from 2 Samuel 7:14. The immediate application in David's experience was to his son, Solomon, whom God would love and discipline as a son (see Ps. 89:27). But the ultimate application is to Jesus Christ, the "greater than Solomon" (Matt. 12:42).

He is the Firstborn who receives worship (v. 6). The term "firstborn" in the Bible does not always mean "born first." God made Solomon the firstborn (Ps. 89:27) even though Solomon is listed *tenth* in the official genealogy (1 Chron. 3:1–5). The title is one of rank and honor, for the firstborn receives the inheritance and the special blessing. Christ is the "Firstborn of all creation" (Col. 1:15 NASB) because He created all things, and He is the highest of all who came back from the dead (Col. 1:18). When He came into the world, the angels worshipped Him (quoted from Deut. 32:43 in the LXX: "Heavens, rejoice with him, let the sons of God pay him homage!"). God commanded them to do so, which proves that Jesus Christ is God, for none of God's angels would worship a mere creature.

He is served by the angels (v. 7). This is a quotation from Psalm 104:4. The Hebrew and Greek words for "spirit" are also translated "wind." Angels are created spirits; they have no bodies, though they can assume human forms when ministering on earth. Angels sometimes served our Lord when He was on earth (Matt. 4:11; Luke 22:43), and they serve Him and us now.

He is God enthroned and anointed (vv. 8–9). In some false cults this quotation from Psalm 45:6 is translated, "Thy divine throne," because cultists dislike this strong affirmation that Jesus Christ is God. But the translation must stand: "Thy throne, O God, is for ever and ever." Angels minister *before* the throne; they do not *sit* on the throne. One of the main teachings of Psalm 110 is that Jesus Christ, God's Anointed (Messiah, Christ), is now enthroned in glory. Jesus Himself referred to this important psalm (Mark 12:35–37; 14:62), and Peter used it on the day of Pentecost (Acts 2:34–36). Our Lord has not yet entered into His earthly kingdom, but He has been enthroned in glory (Eph. 1:20).

When Christ ascended and entered the heavenly glory, He was anointed for His heavenly ministry with "the oil of gladness" (Heb. 1:9). This probably refers to Psalm 16:11, which Peter referred to at Pentecost: "Thou shalt make me full of joy with thy countenance" (Acts 2:28). What a joyful scene that must have been! Psalm 45 is a wedding psalm, and our Lord today is the heavenly Bridegroom who experiences "the joy that was set before him" (Heb. 12:2). Angels praise Him, but they cannot share that position or that joy. Our Lord's throne is forever, which means He is eternal God.

He is the eternal Creator (vv. 10–12). This long quotation comes from Psalm 102:25–27. The angels did not found the earth, for they too are a part of creation. Jesus Christ is the Creator, and one day He will do away with the old creation and bring in a new creation. Everything around us changes, but He will never change. He is "the same yesterday, and to day, and for ever" (Heb. 13:8). Creation is like an old garment, which will one day be discarded in favor of a new one.

Christ is the Sovereign; angels are the servants (vv. 13–14). Again, the writer quotes Psalm 110:1. The fact that Jesus Christ is now at the Father's right hand (the place of honor) is mentioned many times in the New Testament (see Matt. 22:43–44; 26:64; Mark 16:19; Acts 2:33–34; Rom. 8:34; Col. 3:1; Heb. 1:3, 13; 8:1; 10:12; 12:2; 1 Peter 3:22). Angels are the ministering spirits who serve the Lord seated on the throne. But they also minister to us who are the "heirs of salvation" through faith in Christ. The angels today are serving us!

It would be impossible to do away with the evidence presented in these quotations. Jesus Christ is greater than the angels, and this means He is also greater than the law, which they helped deliver to the people of Israel.

2. ADMONITION: HEED THE WORD AND DON'T DRIFT (2:1–4)

This is the first of the five admonitions found in Hebrews. Their purpose is to encourage all readers to pay attention to God's Word and obey it. We have already noted that these admonitions become stronger as we progress through the book, from *drifting* from God's Word to *defying* God's Word (Heb. 12:14–29). We also noted that God does not sit idly by and permit His children to rebel against Him. He will continue to speak and, when necessary, He chastens His own.

The admonition is written to believers, for the writer included himself when he wrote "we." The danger here is that of *neglecting our salvation.*

Please note that the author did not write "rejecting" but "neglecting." He was not encouraging sinners to become Christians; rather, he was encouraging Christians to pay attention to the great salvation they have received from the Lord.

"Lest … we should let them slip" (Heb. 2:1) might better be translated "lest we drift away from them." Later (Heb. 6:19), the writer will use the illustration of an anchor to show how confident we can be in the promises of God. More spiritual problems are caused by neglect than perhaps by any other failure on our part. We neglect God's Word, prayer, worship with God's people (see Heb. 10:25), and other opportunities for spiritual growth, and as a result, we start to drift. The anchor does not move; we do.

During the Old Testament days, people who did not heed the Word were sometimes punished. That Word was given through angels, so how much greater responsibility do we have today who have received the Word from the Son of God! In Hebrews 2:2, "transgression" refers to sins of commission, while "disobedience" suggests sins of omission.

I have often told the story of the pastor who preached a series of sermons on "the sins of the saints." He was reprimanded by a member of the church. "After all," said the member, "sin in the life of a Christian is different from sin in the lives of other people."

"Yes," replied the pastor, "it's worse!"

We have the idea that believers today "under grace" can escape the chastening hand of God that was so evident "under law." But to whom much is given, much shall be required (see Luke 12:48). Not only have we received the Word from the Son of God, but that Word has been confirmed by apostolic miracles (Heb. 2:4). The phrase "signs and wonders" is found eleven times in the New Testament. Here it refers to the miracles that witnessed to the Word and gave confirmation that it was true. These miracles were performed by the apostles (see Mark 16:17–20; Acts 2:43). Today we have the completed Word of God, so there is no need for these apostolic miracles. God now bears witness through His Spirit using the Word (Rom. 8:16; 1 John 5:1–13). The Spirit also gives spiritual gifts to God's people so that they may minister in the church (1 Cor. 12; Eph. 4:1ff.).

Too many Christians today take the Word of God for granted and neglect it. In my pastoral ministry, I have discovered that neglect of the Word of God and prayer, publicly and privately, is the cause of most "spiritual drifting." I need not multiply examples because every believer knows that this is true. He has either experienced this "drifting" or has seen it in the lives of others.

The next time you sing "Come, Thou Fount of Every Blessing," recall that the composer, Robert Robinson, was converted under the mighty preaching of George Whitefield, but that later he drifted from the Lord. He had been greatly used as a pastor, but neglect of spiritual things led him astray. In an attempt to find peace, he began to travel. During one of his journeys, he met a young woman who was evidently very spiritually minded.

"What do you think of this hymn I have been reading?" she asked Robinson, handing him the book. *It was his own hymn!* He tried to avoid her question but it was hopeless, for the Lord was speaking to him. Finally, he broke down and confessed who he was and how he had been living away from the Lord.

"But these 'streams of mercy' are still flowing," the woman assured him, and through her encouragement, Robinson was restored to fellowship with the Lord.

It is easy to drift with the current, but it is difficult to return against the stream. Our salvation is a "great salvation," purchased at a great price. It brings with it great promises and blessings, and it leads to a great inheritance in glory. How can we neglect it?

3. EXPLANATION: WHY JESUS CHRIST IS NOT INFERIOR BECAUSE OF HIS HUMANITY (2:5–18)

The fact that angels are "ministering spirits" without human bodies would seem to give them an advantage over Jesus Christ, who had a human body while He ministered on earth. (Today He has a glorified body that knows no limitations.) The writer gave four reasons that explain why our Lord's humanity was neither a handicap nor a mark of inferiority.

(1) His humanity enabled Him to regain man's lost dominion (vv. 5–9). The quotation here is from Psalm 8:4–6, and you will want to read that entire psalm carefully. When God created the first man and woman, He gave them dominion over His creation (Gen. 1:26–31). David marveled that God would share His power and glory with feeble man! Man was created "a little lower than the angels" (and therefore inferior to them), but man was given privileges far higher than the angels. God never promised the angels that they would reign in "the world to come" (Heb. 2:5).

But we have a serious problem here, for it is obvious that man today is *not* exercising dominion over creation. Certainly man cannot control the fish, fowl, or animals. In fact, man has a hard time controlling himself! "But now we see not yet all things put under him" (Heb. 2:8).

"But we see Jesus" (Heb. 2:9)! He is God's answer to man's dilemma. Jesus Christ became man that He might suffer and die for man's sin and restore the dominion that was lost because of sin. When our Lord was here on earth, He exercised that lost dominion. He had dominion over the fish (see Matt. 17:24–27; Luke 5:1–11; John 21:1–11), over the fowl (Luke 22:34, 60), and over the wild beasts (Mark 1:12–13), and the domesticated beasts (Mark 11:1–7). As the last Adam (1 Cor. 15:45), Jesus Christ regained man's lost dominion. Today, everything is under His feet (Eph. 1:20–23).

Man was "crowned ... with glory and honor" (Heb. 2:7 NASB), but he lost his crown and became the slave of sin. Jesus Christ has regained that "glory and honour" (Heb. 2:9), and believers today share His kingly dominion (Rev. 1:5–6). One day, when He establishes His kingdom, we shall reign with Him in glory and honor. Jesus Christ did all of this for us—for lost sinners—because of "the grace of God" (Heb. 2:9). If He had not become man, He could not have died and "taste[d] death [experienced death] for every man" (Heb. 2:9). It is true that angels cannot die, but it is also true that angels cannot save lost sinners and restore man's lost dominion.

(2) His humanity enabled Him to bring many sons to glory (vv. 10–13). Christ is not only the Last Adam, but He is also the Captain of salvation. That word *captain* literally means "pioneer—one who opens the way for others to follow." Christ gave up His glory to become man. He regained His glory when He arose and ascended to heaven. Now He shares that glory with all who trust Him for salvation (John 17:22–24). He is bringing many sons and daughters to glory!

Christ is united to us, and we are united to Him: We are spiritually one. In fact, we are His "brethren" (Heb. 2:12). The writer quoted Psalm 22:22—a messianic psalm—in which Christ refers to His church as His brethren. This means we and the Son of God share the same nature and belong to the same family! What a marvel of God's grace!

The writer of Hebrews also quoted Isaiah 8:17–18 from the LXX. The immediate reference, of course, is to the prophet Isaiah and his unique sons who were given significant names (see Isa. 7:3; 8:1–4). But the ultimate reference is to Jesus Christ. Not only are believers His brethren, but we are also His children: "Behold I and the children which God hath given me" (Heb. 2:13). If Jesus Christ had not come to earth and become man, He could not take us from earth to share in His glory. The incarnation, crucifixion, and resurrection must go together. They all lead to glory.

One phrase in Hebrews 2:10 ought to be discussed before we move on: "Make the captain of their salvation perfect through sufferings." This statement does not suggest that Jesus Christ was imperfect when He was here on earth. The word translated "perfect" means "complete, effective, adequate." Jesus could not have become an adequate Savior and High Priest had He not become man and suffered and died.

(3) His humanity enabled Him to disarm Satan and deliver us from death (vv. 14–16). Angels cannot die. Jesus did not come to save angels (note Heb. 2:16); He came to save humans. This meant that He had to take on Himself flesh and blood and become a man. Only then could He die and through His death defeat Satan. The word *destroy* does not mean "annihilate," for it is obvious that Satan is still alive and busy. The word means "render inoperative, make of none effect." Satan is not destroyed, but he is disarmed.

In what sense did Satan have the power of death? The final authority of death is in the hands of our God (Deut. 32:39; Matt. 10:28; Rev. 1:18). Satan can do only that which is permitted by God (Job 1:12; 2:6). But because Satan is the author of sin (John 8:44), and sin brings death (Rom. 6:23), in this sense Satan exercises power in the realm of death. Jesus called him a murderer (John 8:44). Satan uses the fear of death as a terrible weapon to gain control over the lives of people. His kingdom is one of darkness and death (Col. 1:13). We who trust in Jesus Christ have once and for all been delivered from Satan's authority and from the terrible fear of death. The death, burial, and resurrection of Christ have given us victory (1 Cor. 15:55–58)!

Jesus Christ did not take on Himself the nature of angels in order to save the fallen angels (2 Peter 2:4; Rev. 12:7–9). Instead, He stooped lower than the angels to become man! And not just "man" in general; but He became a Jew, a part of the "seed of Abraham" (Heb. 2:16). The Jews were a despised and hated race, and yet our Lord became a Jew.

(4) His humanity enables Him to be a sympathetic High Priest to His people (vv. 17–18). Being pure spirits who have never suffered, the angels cannot identify with us in our weaknesses and needs. But Jesus can! While He was here on earth, Jesus was "made like unto his brethren" in that He experienced the sinless infirmities of human nature. He knew what it was to be a helpless baby, a growing child, a maturing adolescent. He knew the experiences of weariness, hunger, and thirst (John 4:6–8). He knew what it was to be despised and rejected, to be lied about and falsely accused. He experienced physical suffering and death. All of this was a part of His "training" for His heavenly ministry as High Priest.

If you want an example of a man who was *not* a merciful and faithful high priest, then read the account about Eli (1 Sam. 2:27–36). Here was a high priest who did not even lead his own sons into a faithful walk with God. Eli even accused brokenhearted Hannah of being drunk (1 Sam. 1:9–18)!

Jesus Christ is both merciful and faithful: He is merciful toward people and faithful toward God. He can never fail in His priestly ministries. He made the necessary sacrifice for our sins so that we might be reconciled to God. He did not need to make a sacrifice for Himself, because He is sinless.

But what happens when we who have been saved are tempted to sin? He stands ready to help us! He was tempted when He was on earth, but no temptation ever conquered Him. Because He has defeated every enemy, He is able to give us the grace that we need to overcome temptation. The word *succour* (Heb. 2:18) literally means "to run to the cry of a child." It means "to bring help when it is needed." Angels are able to *serve* us (Heb. 1:14), but they are not able to *succour* us in our times of temptation. Only Jesus Christ can do that, and He can do it because He became a man and suffered and died.

It might be good at this point to explain the difference between our Lord's ministry as High Priest and His ministry as Advocate (1 John 2:1).

As our High Priest, our Lord is able to give us grace to keep us from sinning when we are tempted. If we do sin, then He as our Advocate represents us before the throne of God and forgives us when we sincerely confess our sins to Him (1 John 1:5—2:2). Both of these ministries are involved in His present work of intercession, and it is this intercessory ministry that is the guarantee of our eternal salvation (note that in Heb. 7:25 it is *"to* the uttermost"—i.e., eternally—and not *"from* the uttermost").

As you review this section, you cannot help but be amazed at the grace and wisdom of God. From a human point of view, it would seem foolish for God to become man, yet it was this very act of grace that made possible our salvation and all that goes with it. When Jesus Christ became man, He did not become inferior to the angels, for in His human body He accomplished something that angels could never accomplish. At the same time, He made it possible for us to share in His glory!

He is not ashamed to call us His brothers and sisters.

Are we ashamed to call Him "Lord"?

QUESTIONS FOR PERSONAL REFLECTION
OR GROUP DISCUSSION

1. What kinds of jobs or roles do you think angels have in our world today?

2. If a child asked you, "How can Jesus be God and still be God's Son?" how would you explain it?

3. In what ways do you, or people you have observed, neglect their salvation?

4. Why is it sometimes difficult to appreciate and pay attention to the Word of God as we should?

5. In what ways is being a human better than being an angel? In what ways do you think being an angel would be better than being a human?

6. In God's infinite wisdom, He surely could have chosen a different way to redeem us. Why do you think He chose becoming a man and dying as a sacrifice?

7. Read Hebrews 4:15. What does it mean to you that Jesus actually experienced life the way you do?

8. Read Philippians 2:5–11. If our attitude is like Christ's, what will our lives be like?

Chapter Three

GREATER THAN MOSES

(Hebrews 3:1—4:13)

Next to Abraham, Moses was undoubtedly the man most greatly revered by the Jewish people. To go back to the law meant to go back to Moses, and the recipients of this letter to the Hebrews were sorely tempted to do just that. It was important that the writer convince his readers that Jesus Christ is greater than Moses, for the entire system of Jewish religion came through Moses. In this section, we learn that Jesus Christ is superior to Moses in at least three respects.

1. CHRIST IS GREATER IN HIS PERSON (3:1–2)

The twofold description of the readers makes it clear that they were converted people. "Holy brethren" could only be applied to people in the family of God, set apart by the grace of God. That the writer was referring to people in the church, the body of Christ, is clear from his use of the phrase "partakers of the heavenly calling." No unconverted Jew or Gentile could ever claim that blessing! The word translated "partakers" here is translated "partners" in Luke 5:7, where it describes the relationship of four men in the fishing business: they were in it together.

True Christians not only share in a heavenly calling, but they also share in Jesus Christ (Heb. 3:14). Through the Holy Spirit, we are "members of his body, of his flesh, and of his bones" (Eph. 5:30). True believers are also "partakers of the Holy Ghost" (Heb. 6:4). "Now if any man have not the Spirit of Christ, he is none of his" (Rom. 8:9). Because we are God's children, we also partake in God's loving chastening (Heb. 12:8). Not to be chastened is evidence that a person is not one of God's children.

Because these people were holy brothers and sisters, and partakers of a heavenly calling, they were able to give a "confession" of their faith in Jesus Christ. The word simply means "to say the same thing." All true Christians "say the same thing" when it comes to their experience of salvation. Twice in this epistle, the writer exhorted the readers to hold fast to this confession (Heb. 4:14; 10:23 NASB). It was this same confession that they were "strangers and pilgrims" on the earth that characterized men and women of faith in the ages past (Heb. 11:13).

It was not Moses who did all of this for the people addressed in this epistle; it was Jesus Christ! The writer did not exhort them to consider Moses, but to consider Christ. The word means "to consider *carefully,* to understand fully." This is no quick glance at Jesus Christ! It is a careful consideration of who He is and what He has done.

That Christ is superior to Moses in His person is an obvious fact. Moses was a mere man, called to be a prophet and leader, while Jesus Christ is the Son of God sent by the Father into the world. The title *apostle* means "one sent with a commission." Moses was called and commissioned by God, but Jesus Christ was *sent* as God's "last Word" to sinful man. You may want to read some of the verses in the gospel of John where Jesus is referred to as "sent from God" (John 3:17, 34; 5:36, 38; 6:29, 57; 7:29; 8:42; 10:36; 11:42; 17:3; and note also 13:3).

Jesus Christ is not only the Apostle, but He is also the High Priest. Moses was a prophet who on occasion served as a priest (see Ps. 99:6), but he was never a high priest. That title belonged to his brother Aaron. In fact, Jesus Christ has the title of Great High Priest (Heb. 4:14).

As the Apostle, Jesus Christ represented God to men, and as the High Priest, He now represents men to God in heaven. Moses, of course, fulfilled similar ministries, for he taught Israel God's truth and he prayed for Israel when he met God on the mount (see Ex. 32:30–32). Moses was primarily the prophet of law, while Jesus Christ is the messenger of God's grace (see John 1:17). Moses helped prepare the way for the coming of the Savior to the earth.

However, the writer of Hebrews noted that Moses and Jesus Christ were *both* faithful in the work God gave them to do. Moses was not sinless, as was Jesus Christ, but he was faithful and obeyed God's will (Num. 12:7). This would be an encouragement to those first-century Jewish believers to remain faithful to Christ, even in the midst of the tough trials they were experiencing. Instead of going back to Moses, they should *imitate* Moses and be faithful in their calling.

2. CHRIST IS GREATER IN HIS MINISTRY (3:3–6)

The word *house* is used six times in these verses. It refers to the people of God, not to a material building. Moses ministered to Israel, the people of God under the old covenant. Today, Christ ministers to His church, the people of God under the new covenant ("whose house are we," Heb. 3:6). You find an illustration of this dual use of "house" in 2 Samuel 7. David wanted to build a temple for God, a house in which God could dwell. But God told David that He would build David's house (household, family) and make a covenant with David's descendants.

The contrast between Moses and Christ is clear: Moses was a *servant in the house,* while Jesus Christ is a *Son over the house.* Moses was a member of the household, but Jesus *built* the house! By the way, the truth in these verses is a powerful argument for the deity of Jesus Christ. If God built all things, and Jesus Christ built God's house, then Jesus Christ must be God.

There is another factor in Christ's superiority over Moses: The prophet Moses spoke about things to come, but Jesus Christ brought the fulfillment of these things (Heb. 3:6). Moses ministered "in the shadows," as it were (see Heb. 8:5 and 10:1), while Jesus Christ brought the full and final light of the gospel of the grace of God.

The Greek word translated "servant" (Heb. 3:5) is not the usual New Testament word for servant or slave. This word carries the meaning of "a voluntary servant who acts because of affection." In the New Testament, it is used only of Moses. At the beginning of his ministry, Moses was a bit hesitant and resisted God's call. But once he surrendered, he obeyed out of a heart of love and devotion.

The "if" clause (Heb. 3:6) needs to be understood in the light of the total context, which is Moses leading Israel out of Egypt and to the Promised Land. The writer is not suggesting that we, as Christians, must keep ourselves saved. This would contradict the major theme of the book, which is the finished work of Christ and His heavenly ministry guaranteeing our eternal salvation (Heb. 7:14ff.). Rather, the writer was affirming that those who hold fast their confidence and hope are proving that they are truly born again.

The word *confidence* literally means "freedom of speech, openness." When you are free to speak, then there is no fear and you have confidence. A believer can come with boldness (synonym of *confidence*) to the throne of grace (Heb. 4:16) with openness and freedom and not be afraid. We have this boldness because of the shed blood of Jesus Christ (Heb. 10:19). Therefore, we should not cast away our confidence, no matter what the circumstances might be. We should not have confidence in ourselves, because we are too prone to fail; but we should have confidence in Jesus Christ who never fails.

Because of this confidence in Christ and this confession of Christ, we can experience joy and hope (Heb. 3:6). The writer exhorted these suffering saints to *enjoy* their spiritual experience and not simply *endure* it. Jesus Christ is the beloved Son over His house, and He will care for each member of the family. He is the faithful High Priest who provides all the grace we need for each demand of life. As the Great Shepherd of the sheep (Heb. 13:19–20), Jesus Christ is using the experiences in His people's lives to equip them for service that will glorify His name.

In other words, those who have trusted Christ *prove* this confession by their steadfastness, confidence, and joyful hope. They are not burdened by the past or threatened by the present, but are "living in the future tense" as they await the "blessed hope" of their Lord's return. It is this "heavenly calling" that motivates the believers to keep on living for the Savior even when the going is tough.

The wandering of Israel in the wilderness is a major topic in this section. Two men in that nation—Caleb and Joshua—illustrate the attitude described in Hebrews 3:6. Everybody else in Israel over the age of twenty was to die in the wilderness and never enter the Promised Land (see Num. 14:26–38). But Caleb and Joshua believed God, and God honored their faith. For forty years, Caleb and Joshua watched their friends and relatives die, but those two men of faith had confidence in God's Word that they would one day enter Canaan. While others were experiencing sorrow and death, Caleb and Joshua rejoiced in confident hope. As believers, we know that God is taking us to heaven, and we should reveal the same kind of joyful confidence and hope.

3. CHRIST IS GREATER IN THE REST HE GIVES (3:7—4:13)
This long section is the second of the five exhortations in this epistle. In the first exhortation (Heb. 2:1–4), the writer pointed out the danger of *drifting*

from the Word because of neglect. In this exhortation, he explained the danger of *doubting* and *disbelieving* the Word because of hardness of heart. It is important that we understand the background of this section, which is the exodus of Israel from Egypt and their experiences of unbelief in the wilderness.

To begin with, we must understand that there are spiritual lessons in the geography of Israel's experiences. The nation's bondage in Egypt is an illustration of a sinner's bondage in this world. Much as Israel was delivered from Egypt by the blood of lambs and the power of God, so a sinner who believes on Christ is delivered from the bondage of sin (Col. 1:13–14). Jesus Christ is "the Lamb of God" whose death and resurrection have made our deliverance from sin a reality.

It was not God's will that Israel remain either in Egypt or in the wilderness. His desire was that the people enter their glorious inheritance in the land of Canaan. But when Israel got to the border of their inheritance, they delayed because they doubted the promise of God (Num. 13—14). "We are not able" wept the ten spies and the people. "We *are* able with God's help!" said Moses, Joshua, and Caleb. Because the people went backward in unbelief instead of forward by faith, they missed their inheritance and died in the wilderness. It was the new generation that possessed the land and entered into their rest.

What does Canaan represent to us as Christians today? It represents our spiritual inheritance in Christ (Eph. 1:3, 11, 15–23). It is unfortunate that some of our hymns and gospel songs use Canaan as a picture of heaven, and "crossing the Jordan" as a picture of death. Since Canaan was a place of battles, and even of defeats, it is not a good illustration of heaven! Israel had to cross the river by faith (a picture of the believer as he dies to self and the world, Rom. 6) and claim the inheritance by faith. They had to "step out by faith" (see Josh. 1:3) and claim the land for themselves, just as believers today must do.

Now we can understand what the wilderness wanderings represent: the experiences of believers who will not claim their spiritual inheritance in Christ, who doubt God's Word and live in restless unbelief. To be sure, God is with them, as He was with Israel, but they do not enjoy the fullness of God's blessing. They are "out of Egypt" but they are not yet "in Canaan."

With this background, we can now better understand one of the key words in this section—*rest* (Heb. 3:11, 18; 4:1, 3–5, 8–11). The writer mentioned two different "rests" found in Old Testament history: (1) *God's Sabbath rest,* when He ceased from His creation activities (Gen. 2:2; Heb. 4:4); (2) *Israel's rest in Canaan* (Deut. 12:9; Josh. 21:43–45; Heb. 3:11). But he saw in these "rests" illustrations of the spiritual experiences of believers today. The Sabbath rest is a picture of our rest in Christ through salvation (Heb. 4:3; see Matt. 11:28). The Canaan rest is a picture of our present rest as we claim our inheritance in Christ (Heb. 4:11–13; note the emphasis on the Word of God). The first is the rest of salvation; the second is the rest of submission.

But there is a third rest that enters into the discussion, that *future rest* that all believers will enjoy with God. "There remaineth therefore a rest to the people of God" (Heb. 4:9). This word for rest is the Greek word *sabbatismos*—"a keeping of a Sabbath"—and this is the only place in the New Testament where this word is used. When the saints enter heaven, it will be like sharing God's great Sabbath rest, with all labors and battles ended (Rev. 14:13).

We may diagram these rests in this way:

Past	*Present*	*Future*
God's Sabbath rest	Salvation rest	Heaven
Israel's Canaan rest	Submission rest	(victory in Christ)

With this background of Israel's history and the "rests" involved, we may now examine the passage itself. The writer gave a threefold admonition.

(1) Let us take heed (3:7–19). Take heed to what? To the sad history of the nation of Israel and the important lesson it teaches. The writer quoted from Psalm 95:7–11, which records God's response to Israel's tragic spiritual condition. God had delivered His people from Egypt and had cared for them, revealing His power in many signs and wonders. Israel saw all of this and benefited from it, but the experience did not bring them closer to God or make them trust Him more. All that God did for them did not benefit them spiritually. In fact, just the opposite took place: They hardened their hearts against God! They put God to the test and He did not fail them, yet they failed Him.

The heart of every problem is a problem in the heart. The people of Israel (except Moses, Joshua, and Caleb) erred in their hearts (Heb. 3:10), which means that their hearts wandered from God and His Word. They also had evil hearts of unbelief (Heb. 3:12); they did not believe that God would give them victory in Canaan. They had seen God perform great signs in Egypt. Yet they doubted He was adequate for the challenge of Canaan.

When a person has an erring heart and a disbelieving heart, the result will also be a hard heart. This is a heart that is insensitive to the Word and work of God. So hard was the heart of Israel that the people even wanted to return to Egypt! Imagine wanting to exchange their freedom under God for slavery in Egypt! Of course, all this history spoke to the hearts of the readers of this letter because they were in danger of "going back" themselves.

God's judgment fell on Israel in the wilderness at Kadesh Barnea. That entire generation was condemned to die, and only the new generation would enter the land. God said, "They shall not enter into my rest" (Heb. 3:11). But what message does this bring to a believer today? No believer today, Jew or Gentile, could go back into the Mosaic legal system since the temple is gone and there is no priesthood. But every believer is tempted to give up his confession of Christ and go back into the world system's life of compromise and bondage. This is especially true during times of persecution and suffering. The fires of persecution have always purified the church because suffering separates true believers from the counterfeit. True believers are willing to suffer for Christ, and they hold firmly to their convictions and their confession of faith (see Heb. 3:6, 14). We are not saved by holding to our confession. The fact that we hold to our confession is proof that we are God's true children.

It is important that we take heed and recognize the spiritual dangers that exist. But it is also important that we encourage each other to be faithful to the Lord (Heb. 3:13). We get the impression that some of these believers addressed were careless about their fellowship in the local assembly (see Heb. 10:23–25). Christians belong to each other and need each other. Moses, Caleb, and Joshua did try to encourage Israel when the nation refused to enter Canaan, but the people would not listen.

It is clear from this section that God was grieved with Israel during the entire forty years they wandered in the wilderness. The Jews had not been out of Egypt long when they began to provoke God (Ex. 16:1ff.). After He supplied bread for them, they complained about a lack of water (Ex. 17:1–7). Moses called that place "Massah and Meribah," which means "provocation and trial." These same words are used in Hebrews 3:10.

The sin of Israel is stated in Hebrews 3:12—"departing from the living God." The Greek word gives us our English word *apostasy*. This is the only place this word is used in Hebrews. Does "apostasy" mean abandoning one's faith and therefore being condemned forever? That does not fit into this context. Israel departed from the living God by refusing God's will for their lives and stubbornly wanting to go their own way back to Egypt. God did not permit them to return to Egypt. Rather, He disciplined them in the wilderness. God did not allow His people to return to bondage.

The emphasis in Hebrews is that true believers have an eternal salvation because they trust a living Savior who constantly intercedes for them. But the writer was careful to point out that this confidence is no excuse for sin. God disciplines His children. Remember that Canaan is not a picture of heaven, but of the believer's present spiritual inheritance in Christ. Believers who doubt God's Word and rebel against Him do not miss heaven, but they do miss out on the blessings of their inheritance today, and they must suffer the chastening of God.

(2) Let us fear (4:1–8). Believers today may enter and enjoy their spiritual inheritance in Christ. We must be careful lest we fail to believe God's Word, for it is only as the Word is "mixed with faith" that it can accomplish its purposes. The argument in this section is given in several propositions: (1) God finished His work and rested, so that His rest has been available since creation; (2) the Jews failed to enter into their rest; (3) many years later (Ps. 95), God said that a rest was still available. That "today" is still here! This means that Joshua did not lead Israel into the true rest, because a rest still remains. (Note that the name "Jesus" in Heb. 4:8 KJV, ought to be "Joshua." "Jesus" is the Greek form of "Joshua.")

The Canaan rest for Israel is a picture of the spiritual rest we find in Christ when we surrender to Him. When we come to Christ by faith, we find salvation rest (Matt. 11:28). When we yield and learn of Him and obey Him by faith, we enjoy submission rest (Matt. 11:29–30). The first is "peace with God" (Rom. 5:1); the second is the "peace of God" (Phil. 4:6–8). It is by believing that we enter into rest (Heb. 4:3); it is by obeying God by faith and surrendering to His will that the rest enters into us.

(3) Let us labor (4:9–13). "Give diligence" is a good translation of this admonition. Diligence is the opposite of "drifting" (Heb. 2:1–3). How do we "give diligence"? By paying close attention to the Word of God. Israel did not believe God's Word, so the rebels fell in the wilderness. "So then faith cometh by hearing, and hearing by the word of God" (Rom. 10:17).

In comparing the Word of God to a sword, the writer was not suggesting that God uses His Word to slaughter the saints! It is true that the Word cuts the heart of sinners with conviction (Acts 5:33; 7:54), and that the Word defeats Satan (Eph. 6:17). The Greek word translated "sword" means "a short sword or dagger." The emphasis is on the power of the Word to penetrate and expose the inner heart of man. The Word is a "discerner" or "critic." The Israelites criticized God's Word instead of allowing the Word to judge them. Consequently, they lost their inheritance.

Of course, God sees our hearts (Heb. 4:13), but we do not always know what is there (Jer. 17:9). God uses the Word to enable us to see the sin and unbelief in our own hearts. The Word exposes our hearts, and then, if we trust God, the Word enables our hearts to obey God and claim His promises. This is why each believer should be diligent to apply himself to hear and heed God's Word. In the Word we see God, and we also see how God sees us. We see ourselves as we really are. This experience enables us to be honest with God, to trust His will, and to obey Him.

All of this is possible because of the finished work of Jesus Christ. (The two "hes" in Heb. 4:10 refer to Jesus Christ.) God rested when He finished the work of creation. God's Son rested when He completed the work of the new creation. We may enter into His rest by trusting His Word and obeying His will. We can do this as we listen to His Word, understand it, trust it, and obey it. Only in this way can we claim our inheritance in Christ.

Before Joshua conquered Jericho, he went out to survey the situation, and he met the Lord Jesus Christ (Josh. 5:13–15). Joshua discovered that he was second in command! The Lord had a sword in His hand, and Joshua fell at His feet in complete submission. It was this action in private that gave Joshua his public victory.

We, too, claim our spiritual inheritance by surrendering to Him and trusting His Word. We must beware of an evil heart of unbelief.

QUESTIONS FOR PERSONAL REFLECTION
OR GROUP DISCUSSION

1. Read Exodus 3:1–13 and John 14:6–14. List some differences between the ways Jesus and Moses accepted their calls.

2. What kinds of tasks or jobs do you think we will perform as rulers with Jesus in the new heaven and earth?

3. The shed blood of Christ allows us to come boldly before God's throne. Is that the way you approach God? If not, what holds you back?

4. Wiersbe says, "The writer exhorted these suffering saints to enjoy their spiritual experience and not simply endure it." What are the signs of someone simply enduring their spiritual experience?

5. When you fall short in your spiritual walk, is it more a product of drifting, doubting, or disbelieving? What makes you say that?

6. The Israelites fought many battles to take control of their home-land. What kinds of struggles do we have that would be the modern equivalent?

7. In what ways would you like to have more "rest" in your spiritual life?

8. Why do we choose to wander through the wilderness when Christ's death allows us to enter His rest in Canaan?

9. What about this world will you most look forward to resting from in heaven?

Chapter Four

GREATER THAN AARON THE HIGH PRIEST

(Hebrews 4:14—5:10)

Moses did not lead the people of Israel into the promised rest; in fact, he himself was forbidden to enter the land. Joshua led them into their *physical* rest, but not into the promised *spiritual* rest (see Heb. 4:8). But what about Aaron, the first high priest? Is it possible that the Aaronic priesthood, with all of its sacrifices and ceremonies, could bring a troubled soul into rest?

The Hebrew Christians who received this letter were sorely tempted to return to the religion of their fathers. After all, any Jew could travel to Jerusalem and *see* the temple and the priests ministering at the altar. Here was something real, visible, concrete. When a person is going through persecution, as these Hebrew Christians were, it is much easier to walk by sight than by faith. Some of us have doubted the Lord under much less provocation than these people were enduring.

The central theme of Hebrews is the priesthood of Jesus Christ, what He is now doing in heaven on behalf of His people. Is the high priestly ministry of Christ superior to that of Aaron and his successors? Yes, it is, and the writer proves his assertion by presenting four arguments.

1. Jesus Christ Has a Superior Title (Heb. 4:14–16)

"Seeing then that we have a *Great* High Priest" (Heb. 4:14). Aaron was a "high priest," but Jesus Christ is the *Great* High Priest. No Old Testament priest could assume that title. But in what does our Lord's greatness consist?

To begin with, Jesus Christ is both God and man. He is "Jesus, the Son of God." The name *Jesus* means "Savior" and identifies His humanity and His ministry on earth. "Son of God" affirms His deity and the fact that He is God. In His unique person, Jesus Christ unites deity and humanity, so that He can bring people to God and bring to people all that God has for them.

Not only in His *person,* but also in His *position,* Jesus Christ is great. Aaron and his successors ministered in the tabernacle and temple precincts, once a year entering the Holy of Holies. But Jesus Christ has "passed through the heavens" (Heb. 4:14, literal translation). When He ascended to the Father, Jesus Christ passed through the atmospheric heavens and the planetary heavens into the third heaven where God dwells (2 Cor. 12:2). How much better is it to have a High Priest who ministers in a heavenly tabernacle than in an earthly one!

But there is another aspect to Christ's position: Not only is He in heaven, but He is *enthroned.* His throne is "the throne of grace" (Heb. 4:16). The mercy seat on the ark of the covenant was God's throne in Israel (Ex. 25:17–22), but it could never be called "a throne of grace." Grace does not veil itself from the people. Grace does not hide itself in a tent.

Furthermore, the common people were not permitted to enter the holy precincts of the tabernacle and the temple, and the priests got only as far as the veil. The high priest alone went beyond the veil, and only on the Day of Atonement (Lev. 16). But *every believer* in Christ is invited, and is even encouraged, to "come boldly unto the throne of grace"! What a great throne it is because our Great High Priest is ministering there.

Jesus Christ, our Great High Priest, is enthroned in heaven. Something else makes Him great: He is ministering mercy and grace to those who come for help. *Mercy* means that God does not give us what we do deserve; *grace* means that He gives us what we do not deserve. No Old Testament high priest could minister mercy and grace in quite the same way. When an Israelite was tempted, he could not easily run to the high priest for help, and he certainly could not enter the Holy of Holies for God's help. But as believers in Jesus Christ, we can run to our High Priest at any time, in any circumstance, and find the help that we need.

Now because of the superiority of Jesus Christ, the Great High Priest, over Aaron, two important conclusions can be drawn. First, there is no need in giving up our profession just because we are going through testing and trial (Heb. 4:14). The word translated "profession" means "confession." These Hebrew Christians were tempted to give up their confession of faith in Christ and their confidence in Him (see Heb. 3:6, 14). It was not a matter of giving up their salvation, since salvation through Christ is eternal (Heb. 5:9). It was a matter of their public confession of faith. By returning to the Old Testament system, they would be telling everyone that they had no faith in Christ (see Gal. 2:11–21). This kind of unbelief would only bring reproach to Christ's name.

After all, the great purpose of salvation is the glory of God (see Eph. 1:6, 12, 14). It was the glory of God that so concerned Moses when Israel broke God's law and made the golden calf (Ex. 32). God offered to destroy the nation and to begin a new one from Moses, but Moses refused the offer. Instead Moses interceded for Israel on the basis of God's glory and God's promise, and God spared the people, even though He disciplined them for their sin (Ex. 32:11–13).

The second conclusion is this: There is no need to go back because we can come boldly into the presence of God and get the help we need

(Heb. 4:16). No trial is too great, no temptation is too strong, but that Jesus Christ can give us the mercy and grace that we need, when we need it. "But He is so far away!" we may argue. "And He is the perfect Son of God! What can He know about the problems of weak sinners like us?"

But that is a part of His greatness! When He was ministering on earth in a human body, He experienced all that we experience, *and even more.* After all, a sinless person would feel temptations and trials in a much greater way than you and I could ever feel them. Christ was tempted, yet He did not sin, and He is able to help us when we are tempted. If we fail to hold fast our confession, we are not proving that Jesus Christ has failed. We are only telling the world that *we failed* to draw on His grace and mercy when it was freely available to us.

2. Jesus Christ Has a Superior Ordination (5:1, 4–6)

When I became pastor of the Calvary Baptist Church in Covington, Kentucky, it was necessary for me to go to the city hall and be bonded. Otherwise, I would not have the authority to perform marriages. I had to show my ordination certificate and prove that I was indeed ministering at the church.

One day I received a frantic phone call from one of our members. Some Christian friends were being married the next day by a relative from Michigan, and they discovered that he was not authorized to perform the ceremony! Could I help them? The visiting pastor could read the ceremony as well as I could, and he knew the couple better than I did, but he lacked the authority to minister.

No man could appoint himself as a priest, let alone as *high* priest. King Saul invaded the priesthood and lost his kingdom (1 Sam. 13). Korah and his fellow rebels tried to make themselves priests, and God judged them (Num. 16). When King Uzziah tried to enter the temple and burn incense, God smote him with leprosy (2 Chron. 26:16–21).

Aaron was chosen by God to be the high priest, and he was duly ordained and installed in office (Ex. 28). He was chosen *from* men to minister *for* men. His main task was at the altar: to offer the sacrifices God had appointed (see Heb. 8:3–4; 9:14). Unless the sacrifices were offered in the right place, by the right person, they were not accepted by God.

The very existence of a priesthood and a system of sacrifices gave evidence that man is estranged from God. It was an act of grace on God's part that He instituted the whole Levitical system. Today, that system is fulfilled in the ministry of Jesus Christ. He is both the sacrifice and the High Priest who ministers to God's people on the basis of His once-for-all offering on the cross.

The subject of ordination stated in Hebrews 5:1 is further developed in Hebrews 5:5–6. Jesus Christ did not appoint Himself as High Priest. He was appointed by God the Father. The quotation in Hebrews 5:5 is from Psalm 2:7. This psalm was already quoted in Hebrews 1:5 to prove that Jesus Christ is the Son of God. But the emphasis in Hebrews 5:5 is on the priesthood of Jesus Christ, not on His deity. What significance, then, does this quotation have for the argument?

The answer to that question is in Acts 13:33–34, where the apostle Paul quoted Psalm 2:7 and explained what it means. The phrase, "This day have I begotten thee," does not refer to the birth of Christ at Bethlehem, but to *His resurrection from the dead.* The Son of God was "begotten" into a glorious new life in His resurrection! He ascended to heaven in a glorified body to become our High Priest at the throne of grace. When Aaron was ordained to the priesthood, he offered the sacrifices of animals. But Jesus Christ, to become our High Priest, offered the sacrifice of Himself—and then arose from the dead!

But God the Father not only said, "Thou art my Son" in Psalm 2:7; He also said, "Thou art a priest forever after the order of Melchizedek" (Heb. 5:6, quoted from Ps. 110:4). This psalm was also quoted earlier in Hebrews

(1:13) to affirm Jesus Christ's final victory over all His enemies. When Aaron was ordained, God did not speak directly to him and declare his priesthood. But the Father did make this special declaration concerning His Son.

Two factors make Christ's priesthood unique and, therefore, His ordination greater. First, He is a High Priest *forever.* No Old Testament priest ministered forever, because each priest died and relinquished the office to his successor. The word *forever* is an important one in this epistle. At least six times the writer affirmed that Christ's high priesthood is forever (Heb. 5:6; 6:20; 7:17, 21, 24, 28). And, since He is a Priest forever, He gives His people salvation forever (Heb. 7:23–28).

The second factor that makes Christ's ordination unique is that He belongs to *a different order* from the Old Testament priests. They belonged to the order of Aaron; He belongs to the order of Melchizedek. This is a key concept in Hebrews, so we must take time to examine and understand it.

Melchizedek is mentioned in only two places in the entire Old Testament—Genesis 14:17–24 and Psalm 110:4. His name means "King of Righteousness," and he was also "King of Salem [peace]." But the fascinating thing about Melchizedek is that he was *both a priest and a king!* King Uzziah wanted to be both a priest and a king, and God judged him. Only in Jesus Christ and in pre-law Melchizedek were these two offices combined. Jesus Christ is a High Priest *on a throne!*

The reason Jesus Christ can be "a priest forever" is that He belongs to the "order of Melchizedek." As far as the Old Testament record is concerned, Melchizedek did not die (see Heb. 7:1–3). Of course, because he was a real man, he did die at some time, but the record is not given to us. So Melchizedek becomes a picture of our Lord Jesus Christ who is a Priest forever.

But Melchizedek also pictures our Lord as a *heavenly* High Priest. Jesus Christ could never have served as a priest when He was on earth because He did not belong to the tribe of Levi. Jesus was born of the seed of David, the tribe of Judah. He became the sacrifice on earth that He might become the High Priest in heaven. All of these truths will be developed in Hebrews 7—10, but they are introduced here.

3. JESUS CHRIST REVEALS A SUPERIOR SYMPATHY (5:2, 7–8)

Every Old Testament high priest had to minister to people who were "ignorant, and … out of the way [wayward]" (Heb. 5:2). God made no provision but judgment for high-handed sins of rebellion (see Ex. 21:12–14; Num. 15:27–31). But He did make provision when people sinned through ignorance or weakness. An Old Testament priest could identify with the sinners, since he himself was a sinner. In fact, on the Day of Atonement, the high priest had to offer a sacrifice *for himself* before he could offer one for the nation (Lev. 16; Heb. 9:7)!

You would think that one sinner would have compassion for another sinner, but this is not always the case. Sin makes a person selfish. Sin can blind us to the hurts of others. Sin can harden our hearts and make us judgmental instead of sympathetic. Remember how heartbroken Hannah, who was praying for a son, was accused by high priest Eli of being drunk (1 Sam. 1:9–18)? And when King David was confronted with a story of a rich man's sin, he had no sympathy for him, even though David himself was a worse sinner (2 Sam. 12).

No, it is the spiritually minded person with a clean heart who sympathizes with a sinner and seeks to help him (see Gal. 6:1). Because we are so sinful, we have a hard time helping other sinners, but because Jesus is perfect, He is able to meet our needs after we sin.

Our Lord was prepared for His high priestly ministry during His days of ministry on earth (Heb. 5:7–8). The phrase "in the days of his flesh" means "in the days when He was on earth in a human body." From birth to death, our Lord experienced the sinless infirmities of human nature. He knew what it was to grow and mature (Luke 2:52). He experienced hunger and thirst, as well as weariness (John 4:6–8, 31). He also faced temptations to sin (Matt. 4:1–11) and persecutions from the hands of sinful men.

How could the Son of God "learn obedience"? In the same way any son must learn obedience: by the experiences of life. We must remember that our Lord, in His earthly walk, lived by faith in the Father's will. As God, He needed to learn nothing. But as the Son of God come in human flesh He had to experience that which His people would experience so that He might be able to minister as their High Priest. He did not need to learn *how* to obey because it would be impossible for God to be disobedient. Rather, as the God-man in human flesh, He had to learn what was involved in obedience. In this way, He identified with us.

This preparation involved the experience of death. The writer of Hebrews (5:7) focused on our Lord's experience in the garden of Gethsemane (Matt. 26:36–46). As He faced the cross, it was not the physical suffering that burdened Jesus, but the fact that He would be made sin and separated from His Father (2 Cor. 5:21; 1 Peter 2:24). Other servants of God have faced death and not expressed such great emotion; but no other servant ever bore on his body the sins of the whole world.

In His Gethsemane prayer, our Lord did not oppose the Father, but prayed, "Not my will, but thine, be done" (Luke 22:42). He was not praying to be spared *from* death, but to be saved *out of death.* He was praying for resurrection from the dead, and God answered that prayer. He had prophesied His own death and had made it clear that He was laying down His life of His own free will. This ties in with the quotation from Psalm 2:7, cited in Hebrews 5:5, that promised His resurrection from the dead.

The writer of Hebrews states that Jesus' prayer "was heard" (Heb. 5:7), that is, answered by the Father. Since He *did* die on the cross, this could not have been what He was praying about; for if the Father had answered, the

Son would not have been crucified. He did not pray to be saved *from* death, but *out of death*, and God answered His prayer by raising Him from the dead.

No one else ever died the kind of death that Jesus died. He was made sin for us. Men have died because of their own sins, but only Jesus died for the sins of a whole world. He experienced the ultimate in suffering and, therefore, He is able to sympathize with His people when they are suffering. The readers of this epistle were going through difficult times, but they had "not yet resisted unto blood" (Heb. 12:4). Their goods had been seized and they had been ridiculed (Heb. 10:32–34), but they had not been crucified and forsaken by the Father.

No matter what trials we meet, Jesus Christ is able to understand our needs and help us. We need never doubt His ability to sympathize and strengthen. It is also worth noting that sometimes God puts us through difficulties that we might better understand the needs of others, and become able to encourage them (see 2 Cor. 1:8ff.).

When Charles Haddon Spurgeon was a young preacher in London, his successful ministry aroused the envy of some of the clergy, and they attacked him with various kinds of slander and gossip. His sermons were called "trashy," and he was called "an actor" and "a pulpit buffoon." Even after his ministry was established, Spurgeon was lied about in the press (including the *religious* press), and this was bound to discourage him.

After one particularly scurrilous report in the press, Spurgeon fell before the Lord and prayed, "O Lord Jesus, Thou didst make Thyself of no reputation for me. I willingly lay my reputation down for Thy sake." From that time on, Spurgeon had peace in his heart. He knew that his Great High Priest understood his need and would give him the grace that he needed for each hour.

4. Jesus Christ Offered a Superior Sacrifice (5:3, 9–10)

This topic has already been touched on, and the writer of Hebrews discusses it in detail in Hebrews 9—10. Two important matters are involved.

The first is that Jesus Christ did not need to offer any sacrifices for Himself. On the annual Day of Atonement, the high priest first had to sacrifice for himself, and then he could offer the sacrifices for his nation (Lev. 16). Since Jesus is the sinless Son of God, there was no need for Him to sacrifice for Himself. He was in perfect fellowship with the Father and needed no cleansing.

The second matter is that our Lord's sacrifice was once and for all, whereas the Old Testament sacrifices had to be repeated. Furthermore, those sacrifices could only *cover* sins; they could never *cleanse* sins. It required the sacrifice of the spotless Lamb of God for sin to be cleansed and removed.

Because He is the sinless, eternal Son of God, and because He offered a perfect sacrifice, Jesus Christ is the "author of eternal salvation" (Heb. 5:9). No Old Testament priest could offer *eternal* salvation to anyone, but that is exactly what we have in Jesus Christ. The phrase "being made perfect" does not suggest that Jesus was imperfect! The word means "made complete"; we described it in our study of Hebrews 2:10. By means of His earthly sufferings, Jesus Christ was equipped for His heavenly ministry as our High Priest. He is able to save, keep, and strengthen His people.

Does the phrase "them that obey him" (Heb. 5:9) suggest that, if we do not obey Him, we may lose that eternal salvation? To "obey God" is the same as "to trust God," as "them that obey him" is a description of those who have put their faith in Jesus Christ. "A great company of the priests were obedient to the faith" (Acts 6:7). "But they have not all obeyed the gospel" (Rom. 10:16). "Ye have purified your souls in obeying the truth"

(1 Peter 1:22). Once we have put our faith in Jesus Christ, and thus obeyed His call, we experience His eternal salvation.

It is difficult to resist the four arguments presented in this section. We must conclude with the writer that Jesus Christ the Great High Priest is superior to Aaron. It would be foolish for anyone to return to the inferiorities of the old law when he could enjoy the superiorities of Jesus Christ. Then why were these Hebrew believers tempted to go back into legalism? *Because they were not going on to maturity in Christ!* For this reason the writer paused to exhort them to grow up in the Lord, and that is the theme for our next chapter.

QUESTIONS FOR PERSONAL REFLECTION
OR GROUP DISCUSSION

1. When you think of a restful place, what images come to your mind?

2. If you could have the ideal priest, what would his traits be?

3. Do you frequently approach the throne of grace with confidence? Why or why not?

4. Picture Jesus praying to the Father as Hebrews 5:7 describes. How was His prayer life like yours? How was it different?

5. Wiersbe writes, "*Mercy* means that God does not give us what we do deserve; *grace* means that He gives us what we do not deserve." How have you seen mercy and grace displayed in your life?

6. In what ways do you interact with Christ as your Priest? As your King?

7. Why is it difficult sometimes to grant mercy to someone else, even though we sin ourselves?

8. Think of a time when you have felt separate or distant from God. Describe what you think it was like for Christ to be separate from God on the cross.

9. How does it feel to be accused or punished for something you didn't do (as Christ was in His death)? Why did Christ go through that willingly?

10. What element of Christ's sacrifice as your High Priest touches you the most?

Chapter Five

PILGRIMS SHOULD MAKE PROGRESS

(Hebrews 5:11—6:20)

W e do not want you to become lazy, but to imitate those who through faith and patience inherit what has been promised" (Heb. 6:12 NIV).

This verse summarizes the main message of this difficult (and often misunderstood) section of the epistle. Israel wanted to go back to Egypt, and, as a result, a whole generation failed to inherit what God had promised. They were safely delivered out of Egypt, but they never enjoyed the promised rest in Canaan. We believers today can make the same mistake.

If you keep in mind that the emphasis in this section is on *making spiritual progress,* you will steer safely through misinterpretations that could create problems. In this section, the writer deals with three topics that relate to spiritual progress.

1. THE MARKS OF SPIRITUAL IMMATURITY (5:11–14)

The writer was about to begin his explanation of the heavenly priesthood of Christ, but he was not sure his readers were ready for what he had to teach. The problem was not that he is a dull teacher, but that they were dull hearers! The word translated "dull" in Hebrews 5:11 is translated "slothful" in Hebrews 6:12. It refers to a condition of spiritual apathy and laziness that prevents spiritual development.

What, then, are the marks of spiritual immaturity?

Dullness toward the Word (v. 11). These believers started on their "backward journey" by *drifting from the Word* (Heb. 2:1–4), and then *doubting the Word* (Heb. 3:7—4:13). As a result, they were now "dull of hearing"; that is, unable to listen to the Word, receive it, and act on it. They did not have the attitude of the Thessalonians: "For this cause also thank we God without ceasing, because, when ye received the word of God which ye heard of us, ye received it not as the word of men, but as it is in truth, the word of God, which effectually worketh also in you that believe" (1 Thess. 2:13).

One of the first symptoms of spiritual regression, or backsliding, is a dullness toward the Bible. Sunday school class is dull, the preaching is dull, anything spiritual is dull. The problem is usually not with the Sunday school teacher or the pastor, but with the believer himself.

Inability to share (v. 12a). The ability to share spiritual truth with others is a mark of maturity. Not all Christians have the gift of teaching, but all can share what they learn from the Word. One of the hardest lessons children must learn is the lesson of sharing. The recipients of this letter had been saved long enough to be able to share God's truth with others. But, instead of helping others to grow, these Hebrew Christians were in need of learning *again* the simple teachings of the Christian life. They were experiencing a second childhood!

A "baby food" diet (vv. 12b–13). Milk is predigested food, and it is specially suited to babies. But only those who have teeth can enjoy meat. The writer defines the "milk" as "the first principles of the oracles of God" (Heb. 5:12). The "meat" of the Word is the teaching about our Lord's ministry *now* in heaven as our High Priest. The writer wanted to give this "meat" to them, but they were not ready for it.

The "milk" of the Word refers to what Jesus Christ did on earth—His birth, life, teaching, death, burial, and resurrection. The "meat" of the Word refers to what Jesus Christ is now doing in heaven. We begin the Christian life on the basis of His finished work on earth. We grow in the Christian life on the basis of His unfinished work in heaven.

Of course, even the maturest adult never outgrows milk. As believers, we can still learn much from our Lord's work on earth. *But we must not stop there!* We must make spiritual progress, and we can do this only if we learn about Christ's priestly ministry for us in heaven. (See Heb. 13:20–21 for a summary of what the Lord wants to do for His people now.)

Unskillful in using the Word (v. 14). As we grow in the Word, we learn to use it in daily life. As we apply the Word, we exercise our "spiritual senses" and develop spiritual discernment. It is a characteristic of little children that they lack discernment. A baby will put anything into its mouth. An immature believer will listen to any preacher on the radio or television and not be able to identify whether or not he is true to the Scriptures.

Just as our physical bodies have senses without which we could not function, so our inner "spiritual man" has "spiritual senses." For example, "O taste and see that the Lord is good" (Ps. 34:8); "But blessed are your eyes, for they see: and your ears, for they hear" (Matt. 13:16). As we feed on the Word of God and apply it in daily life, our inner "spiritual senses" get their exercise and become strong and keen. Paul called this process exercising ourselves unto godliness (1 Tim. 4:7–8).

The ability to discern good and evil is a vital part of Christian maturity. The nation of Israel in Moses' day lacked this discernment and failed to claim its promised inheritance. The readers of this letter were in danger of making the same mistake. It is impossible to stand still in the Christian life: We either go forward and claim God's blessing, or we go backward and wander about aimlessly.

I once heard a preacher say, "Most Christians are 'betweeners.'"

"What do you mean by that?" I asked.

"They are between Egypt and Canaan—out of the place of danger, but not yet into the place of rest and rich inheritance," he replied. "They are between Good Friday and Easter Sunday—saved by the blood but not yet enjoying newness of resurrection life."

Are *you* a betweener?

2. THE CALL TO SPIRITUAL MATURITY (6:1–12)

No one can escape coming into the world as a baby, because that is the only way to get here! But it is tragic when a baby fails to mature. No matter how much parents and grandparents love to hold and cuddle a baby, it is their great desire that the baby grow up and enjoy a full life as a mature adult. God has the same desire for His children. That is why He calls to us, "Go on to maturity" (Heb. 6:1 NIV)!

It is a call to spiritual progress (vv. 1–3). If we are going to make progress, we have to leave the childhood things behind and go forward in spiritual growth. Hebrews 6:1 literally reads, "Therefore, having left [once and for all] the elementary lessons [the ABCs] of the teaching of Christ." When I was in kindergarten, the teacher taught us our ABCs. (We didn't have television to teach us in those days.) You learn your ABCs so that you might read words, sentences, books—in fact, anything in literature. But you do not keep learning the basics. You use the basics to go on to better things.

The phrase, "Let us go on," should be translated, "Let us be carried forward." It is God who enables us to progress as we yield to Him, receive His Word, and act on it. A baby does not "grow himself." He grows as he eats, sleeps, exercises, and permits his body to function. Nature, as ordained by God, carries the baby along day after day, and gradually he matures into an adult. It is normal for Christians to grow; it is abnormal for them to have arrested growth.

The writer lists six foundational truths of the Christian life, all of which, by the way, are also foundational to the Jewish faith. After all, our Christian faith is based on the Jewish faith and is a fulfillment of it. "Salvation is of the Jews" (John 4:22). If the readers of this epistle went back to Judaism in order to escape persecution, they would only be abandoning the perfect for the imperfect, the mature for the immature.

The first two items (repentance and faith) are *Godward* and mark the initiation of the spiritual life. To repent means to change one's mind. It is not simply a "bad feeling about sin," because that could be regret or remorse. It is changing one's mind about sin to the point of turning from it. Once a sinner has repented (and this itself is a gift from God, Acts 5:31; 11:18), then he is able to exercise faith in God. Repentance and faith go together (Acts 20:21).

The next two items (baptisms and laying on of hands) have to do with a person's relationship to *the local assembly of believers.* In the New Testament, a person who repented and trusted Christ was baptized and became a part of a local church (Acts 2:41–47). The word *baptisms* in Hebrews 6:2 is plural and can be translated "washings" (Heb. 9:10). While water itself can never cleanse sin (1 Peter 3:21), baptism is a symbol of spiritual cleansing ("Get up, be baptized and wash your sins away, calling on his name" [Acts 22:16 NIV]) as well as our identification with Christ in death, burial, and resurrection (Rom. 6:1–4). The "laying on of hands" (Heb. 6:2) symbolized the sharing of some blessing (Luke 24:50; Acts 19:6) or the setting apart of a person for ministry (1 Tim. 4:14).

The last two items, the resurrection of the dead (Acts 24:14–15) and the final judgment (Acts 17:30–31), have to do with *the future.* Both orthodox Jews and Christians believe in these doctrines. The Old Testament teaches a general resurrection, but does not make the doctrine clear. The New Testament teaches a resurrection of the saved and also a resurrection of the lost (John 5:24–29; Rev. 20:4–6, 12–15).

The lesson of the paragraph (Heb. 6:1–3) is clear: "You have laid the foundation. You know your ABCs. Now move forward! Let God carry you along to maturity!"

This progress does not affect salvation (vv. 4–6). These verses, along with the exhortation in Hebrews 10:26–39, have given people cause for worry and concern, mainly because these verses have been misunderstood and misapplied. I have received long-distance phone calls from upset people who have misread this passage and convinced themselves (or been convinced by Satan) that they were hopelessly lost and had committed some unpardonable sin. While I do not want to give a false assurance to any professed Christian who is not truly born again, neither do I want to cause some true believer to stumble and miss God's best.

Bible students over the years have come up with several approaches to this serious passage. One view is that the writer is warning us against the sin of apostasy, willfully turning one's back on Jesus Christ and returning to the old life. According to them, such a person would be lost forever. I have several problems with this interpretation. To begin with, the Greek word *apostosia* is not used in this passage. The verb for "fall away" (Heb. 6:6) is *parapipto,* which literally means "to fall alongside." Second, we always interpret the obscure by the obvious. There are many verses in Scripture that assure the true believer that he can never be lost. In fact, one of the greatest arguments for security is the last section of this chapter (Heb. 6:13–20; see also John 5:24; 10:26–30; Rom. 8:28–39).

Those who teach that we can lose our salvation also teach that such a person can be restored. But this passage (Heb. 6:4–6) teaches just the opposite! If you omit the intervening clauses, the statement reads: "For it is impossible ... to renew them again unto repentance." In other words, if this refers to apostasy, once a saved person turns his back on Christ, he *cannot* be restored to salvation. He is lost forever.

Others claim that the people addressed were not true believers. They had cooperated with the Holy Spirit up to a point, but were not actually born again. Well, let's examine the description of these people and see if they possessed true salvation.

They were "enlightened" (Heb. 6:4). The "once" means "enlightened once and for all." The way this same verb is used in Hebrews 10:32 indicates an experience of true salvation (see 2 Cor. 4:4–6).

They "tasted of the heavenly gift" (Heb. 6:4b), and "tasted the good word of God, and the powers of the world [age] to come" (Heb. 6:5). To claim that these people "tasted but did not eat" is to base interpretation on one meaning of an English word. God permitted His Son to "taste death for every man" (Heb. 2:9). Surely Jesus Christ did not simply *sample* death on the cross! "Taste" carries the idea of "experience." These Hebrew believers had experienced the gift of salvation, the Word of God, and the power of God. Doesn't this describe authentic salvation?

They "were made partakers of the Holy Ghost" (Heb. 6:4c). To suggest that they only went along with the Holy Spirit to a certain extent is to ignore the simple meaning of the verb. It means "to become sharers." These same people were not only "sharers of the Holy Spirit," but also "partakers of the heavenly calling" (Heb. 3:1) and "partakers of Christ" (Heb. 3:14).

In view of these facts, I have concluded that the people addressed were true believers, not mere professors. Furthermore, how could *unsaved* people ever disgrace Jesus Christ and put Him to open shame?

A third view is that this sin (whatever it is) could be committed only by Hebrew Christians in the first century, while the temple services were still going on. If so, then why did the writer connect this exhortation with the *heavenly* priesthood of our Lord and the importance of spiritual maturity? If what he wrote about cannot happen today, what is the motivation behind the exhortation? It all seems futile to me if we limit these verses to first-century Jewish believers.

Then what is the writer trying to say to us? It is probable that he was describing a *hypothetical case* to prove his point that a true believer cannot lose his salvation. His statement in Hebrews 6:9 seems to support this interpretation: "Even though we speak like this, dear friends, we are confident of better things in your case" (NIV). His argument runs like this: "Let's suppose that you do not go on to maturity. Does this mean that you will go back to condemnation, that you will lose your salvation? Impossible! If you *could* lose your salvation, it would be impossible to get it back again, and this would disgrace Jesus Christ. He would have to be crucified again for you, and this could never happen."

In Hebrews 6:4, the writer changed the pronouns from "we" and "us" to "those." This change also suggests that he had a hypothetical case in mind.

However, there is another possible interpretation that does not require a hypothetical case. You should note that the words *crucify* and *put* in Hebrews 6:6 are, in the Greek, present participles: "while they *are crucifying* … and while they *are putting* him to an open shame." The writer did not say that these people could *never* be brought to repentance. He said that they could not be brought to repentance *while they were treating Jesus Christ in such a shameful way.* Once they stop disgracing Jesus Christ in this way, they can be brought to repentance and renew their fellowship with God.

Whatever approach you take, please keep in mind that the writer's purpose was not to frighten the readers but to assure them. If he had wanted to frighten them, he would have named whatever sin (or sins) would have caused them to disgrace Jesus Christ, but he did not do so. In fact, he avoided the word *apostasy* and used instead "to fall by the wayside" (see Gal. 6:1 for a similar word).

Christians *can* "sin unto death" (1 Cor. 11:30–32; 1 John 5:16–17). This is God's chastening, a theme the writer of Hebrews will take up in Hebrews 12.

This progress results in fruitfulness (vv. 7–10). This illustration of a field reminds us of our Lord's parable of the sower (Matt. 13:1–9, 18–23), as well as Paul's teaching about the fire testing our works (1 Cor. 3:6–23). A field proves its worth by bearing fruit, and a true believer, as he makes spiritual progress, bears fruit for God's glory. Note that the "thorns and briars" are burned, not the field. God never curses His own!

The crop of God's blessing pictured in Hebrews 6:7 is called "things that accompany salvation" in Hebrews 6:9. Not every believer bears the same *amount* of fruit ("some an hundredfold, some sixty, some thirty," Matt. 13:23); but every believer bears the same *kind* of fruit as proof that he is a child of God (Matt. 7:15–20). This is the fruit of Christian character and conduct (Gal. 5:22–26) produced by the Spirit as we mature in Christ.

The writer listed some of the fruit that he knew had been produced in their lives (Heb. 6:10): Because of their love, they had worked and labored for the Lord; they had ministered to other saints; and they were still ministering (see 1 Thess. 1:3–10; Rev. 2:2). These are some of the "things that accompany salvation."

But he was concerned lest they rest on their achievements and not press on to full maturity and the enjoyment of God's rich inheritance.

This progress demands diligent effort (vv. 11–12). While it is true that it is God who carries us along to maturity (Heb. 6:1, 3), it is also true that the believer must do his part. We must not be lazy ("slothful," the same word as "dull" in Heb. 5:11) but apply ourselves to the spiritual resources God has given us. We have the promises from God. We should exercise faith and patience and claim these promises for ourselves! Like Caleb and Joshua, we must believe God's promise and want to go in and claim the land! The illustration of the farm (Heb. 6:7–8) and the admonition to be diligent always remind me of Solomon's warning (Prov. 24:30–34). Read it—*and heed it!*

3. The Basis for Spiritual Security (6:13–20)

Lest anyone should misinterpret his exhortation to spiritual maturity, the writer ended this section with a tremendous argument for the assurance of salvation. All of us Christians are not making the spiritual progress we should, but we need never fear that God will condemn us. The writer gave three arguments for the certain salvation of true believers.

(1) God's promise (vv. 13–15). God's main promise to Abraham is recorded in Genesis 22:16–17. In spite of Abraham's failures and sins, God kept His promise and Isaac was born. Many of God's promises do not depend on our character but on His faithfulness. The phrase "patiently endured" (Heb. 6:15) is the exact opposite of "slothful" (Heb. 6:12). The readers of this letter were about to give up; their endurance was running out (see Heb. 12:1–2). "You will obtain and enjoy what God has promised if you diligently apply yourself to the development of your spiritual life," is what the writer stated.

We Christians today have more of God's promises than did Abraham! What is keeping us from making spiritual progress? *We do not apply ourselves by faith.* To return to the illustration of the farm, the farmer does not reap a harvest by sitting on the porch looking at the seed. He must get busy and plow, plant, weed, cultivate, and perhaps water the soil. The believer who neglects church fellowship, ignores his Bible, and forgets to pray is not going to reap much of a harvest.

(2) God's oath (vv. 16–18). God not only gave Abraham a promise, but He also confirmed that promise with an oath. When a witness takes an oath in court, he is confronted with the words "so help me God." We call on the Greater to witness for the lesser. None is greater than God, so He swore by Himself!

But God did not do this only for Abraham. He has also given His promise and oath to "the heirs of promise" (Heb. 6:17). Abraham and his descendants are the first of these heirs (see Heb. 11:9), but all believers are included as "Abraham's [spiritual] seed" (Gal. 3:29). So our assurance of salvation is guaranteed by God's promise and God's oath, "two immutable [unchangeable] things" (Heb. 6:18). We have "strong consolation" (or "great encouragement") concerning the hope set before us! Hebrews is a book of encouragement, not discouragement!

The phrase "fled for refuge" (Heb. 6:18) suggests the Old Testament "cities of refuge" described in Numbers 35:9ff. and Joshua 20. God appointed six cities, three on each side of the Jordan, into which a man could flee if he had accidentally killed someone. The elders of the city would investigate the case. If they determined that it was indeed manslaughter and not murder, they would permit the man to live in the city until the death of the high priest. Then he could return to his home. The members of the slain man's family could not avenge themselves so long as the man remained in the city.

We have fled to Jesus Christ, and He is our eternal refuge. As our High Priest, He will never die (Heb. 7:23–25), and we have eternal salvation. No avenger can touch us, because He has already died and arisen from the dead.

(3) God's Son (vv. 19–20). Our hope in Christ is like an anchor for the soul. The anchor was a popular symbol in the early church. At least sixty-six pictures of anchors have been found in the catacombs. The Greek stoic philosopher Epictetus wrote, "One must not tie a ship to a single anchor, nor life to a single hope." Christians have but one anchor—Jesus Christ our hope (Col. 1:5; 1 Tim. 1:1).

However, this spiritual anchor is different from material anchors on ships. For one thing, we are anchored *upward*—to heaven—not downward. We are anchored not to stand still, but to *move ahead!* Our anchor is sure—it cannot break—and steadfast—it cannot slip. No earthly anchor can give that kind of security!

The writer then clinched the argument: This Savior is our "forerunner" who has gone ahead to heaven so that we may one day follow (Heb. 6:20)! The Old Testament high priest was *not* a "forerunner" because nobody could follow him into the Holy of Holies. But Jesus Christ has gone to heaven so that one day we may follow.

Dr. H. A. Ironside has suggested that the two phrases "within the veil" (Heb. 6:19) and "without the camp" (Heb. 13:13) summarize the epistle to the Hebrews. Jesus Christ is "within the veil" as our High Priest. We can therefore come boldly to His throne and receive all the help that we need. But we must not be "secret saints." We must be willing to identify with Christ in His rejection and go "without the camp, bearing his reproach" (Heb. 13:13). The Hebrew believers who received this letter were tempted to compromise to avoid that reproach. However, if we live "within the veil," we shall have no trouble going "without the camp."

Regardless of what approach you take to the exhortation in this section, be sure to lay hold of the main lesson: Believers must go on to maturity, and God has made it possible for us to do so. If we start to *drift from the Word* (Heb. 2:1–4), then we will also start to *doubt the Word* (Heb. 3:7—4:13). Before long, we will get *dull toward the Word* (Heb. 5:11—6:20) and become lazy believers. The best way to keep from drifting is to *lay hold of the anchor!*

Anchored heavenward! How much more secure can you be?

QUESTIONS FOR PERSONAL REFLECTION
OR GROUP DISCUSSION

1. How do you know if you are making spiritual progress or not?

2. In what ways can we take responsibility for our own spiritual growth?

3. We often don't realize how far we have fallen away from the Word of God until we have really fallen. How would you describe the very first steps toward becoming dull to God's Word?

4. Put into your own words the difference between the "meat" and "milk" of God's Word.

5. What keeps us in between Egypt and Canaan, Good Friday and Easter Sunday—"saved by the blood but not yet enjoying newness of resurrection life"?

6. Think of people you've known or observed who were strong in their faith but then fell away. How do they fit in with the "falling away" described in this chapter? Did you doubt their salvation?

7. How does it feel to know you are loved unconditionally, to know that your place in someone's life is secure?

8. What would change about your life if you believed you could lose your salvation?

9. List some ways that Jesus has been an anchor for you.

10. What elements of our culture make it easier to drift away from the Word and love of God?

Chapter Six

MYSTERIOUS MELCHIZEDEK

(Hebrews 7)

Ever since a city librarian introduced me to the Sherlock Holmes stories many years ago, I have been a reader of good detective fiction. Of course, I always try to solve the mystery before I get to the final chapter, and sometimes I succeed. This much I have learned: Never overlook *any* character in the story, even the most incidental. He or she may be the criminal.

If you were asked to name the most important people in the Old Testament, I doubt that Melchizedek's name would be on your list. He appeared once, in Genesis 14:17–24, and he was referred to once more, in Psalm 110:4. You could hardly call this "top billing." But the Holy Spirit reached back into the Old Testament and used those two passages to present a most important truth: The priesthood of Jesus Christ is superior to that of Aaron because "the order of Melchizedek" is superior to "the order of Levi."

Chapter 7 of Hebrews introduces the second main section, as we have outlined it: *A Superior Priesthood* (Heb. 7—10). In Hebrews 7, the writer argued that Christ's priesthood, like Melchizedek's, is superior in its *order*. In Hebrews 8, the emphasis is on Christ's better *covenant;* in Hebrews 9, it is His better *sanctuary;* and Hebrews 10 concludes the section by arguing for Christ's better *sacrifice.*

The Jewish nation was accustomed to the priesthood of the tribe of Levi. This tribe was chosen by God to serve in the tabernacle (Ex. 29; Num. 18). Aaron was the first high priest, appointed by God. In spite of their many failures, the priests had served God for centuries, but now the writer has affirmed that their priesthood has ended! To defend this statement, and to prove that the order of Melchizedek is superior to that of Aaron, he presented three arguments.

1. THE HISTORICAL ARGUMENT: MELCHIZEDEK AND ABRAHAM (7:1–10)

The record of the event discussed is in Genesis 14:17–24, so take time to read it. The writer of our epistle wanted us to note several facts about this mysterious man, Melchizedek.

He was both king and priest (v. 1). We have noted already that, in the Old Testament economy, the throne and the altar were separated. Those persons who attempted to invade the priests' office were judged by God. But here is a man who had *both* offices—king and priest! Aaron never had that privilege. And it is important to note that Melchizedek was not a "counterfeit" priest: He was the "priest of the most high God" (Gen. 14:18). His ministry was legitimate.

His name is significant (v. 2b). In the Bible, names and their meanings are often important. We name our children today without much consideration for what their names mean, but this was not the case in Bible days. Sometimes a great spiritual crisis was the occasion for changing a person's name (see Gen. 32:24–32; John 1:35–42). The name *Melchizedek* means "king of righteousness" in the Hebrew language. The word *Salem* means "peace" (the Hebrew word *shalom)*, so that Melchizedek is "king of peace" as well as "king of righteousness."

"Righteousness" and "peace" are often found together in Scripture.

"And the work of righteousness shall be peace; and the effect of righteousness quietness and assurance forever" (Isa. 32:17); "Mercy and truth are met together; righteousness and peace have kissed each other" (Ps. 85:10); "In his days shall the righteous flourish; and abundance of peace so long as the moon endureth" (Ps. 72:7); "But the wisdom that is from above is first pure, then peaceable.... And the fruit of righteousness is sown in peace of them that make peace" (James 3:17–18). Of course, God's purpose for His people is that they bear "the peaceable fruit of righteousness" (Heb. 12:10–11).

True peace can be experienced only on the basis of righteousness. If we want to enjoy "peace with God," we must be "justified [declared righteous] by faith" (Rom. 5:1). Man cannot produce righteousness by keeping the Old Testament law (Gal. 2:21). It is only through the work of Jesus Christ on the cross that righteousness and peace could have "kissed each other."

Melchizedek received tithes from Abraham (v. 2a). This important fact is explained in Hebrews 7:4–10. The word tithe means "one tenth." Under the Jewish law, the Jews were commanded to give God one tenth of their crops, herds, and flocks (Lev. 27:30–32). These tithes were brought to the Levites (Num. 18:21ff.) at the tabernacle and later at the temple (Deut. 12:5ff.). If the trip was too long for transporting grain, fruit, or animals, the tithe could be converted into money (Deut. 14:22–27).

Tithing, however, did not originate with Moses. Abraham practiced tithing long before the law was given. In fact, archaeologists have discovered that other nations also tithed in that day; so the practice is an ancient one.

His family history is different (v. 3). Melchizedek was a man (see Heb. 7:4), so he had to have had a mother and a father. But there is no *record* of his genealogy ("descent") in the Old Testament, and this is significant because most great persons in the Old Testament have their ancestry identified. It was especially important that the priests be able to prove their ancestry (see Ezra 2:61–63; Neh. 7:63–65). Here the writer of Hebrews used an argument from silence, but it is a valid one.

Melchizedek was not an angel or some superhuman creature; nor was he an Old Testament appearance of Jesus Christ. He was a real man, a real king, and a real priest in a real city. But *as far as the record is concerned,* he was not born, nor did he die. In this way, he is a picture of the Lord Jesus Christ, the eternal Son of God. Though Jesus Christ did die, Calvary was not the end, for He arose from the dead and today lives in "the power of an endless life" (Heb. 7:16). Since there is no account of Melchizedek's death, as far as the record is concerned, it seems that Melchizedek is still serving as a priest and king. This is another way in which he is like the eternal Son of God.

The application is clear: Neither Aaron nor any of his descendants could claim to be "without genealogy" (Heb. 7:3 NASB). They could not claim to have an endless ministry. Nor could they claim to be both kings and priests, like Jesus Christ.

He had authority to receive tithes and to bless Abraham (vv. 4–10). The greatness of Melchizedek is seen in the fact that Abraham gave him tithes from the loot of a miniwar. Abraham acknowledged the authority of Melchizedek. Furthermore, Melchizedek blessed Abraham in a special way, and "the less is blessed of the better" (Heb. 7:7). In giving Melchizedek tithes and in receiving his blessing, Abraham affirmed the greatness of this king-priest.

But how does this relate to Aaron? In an interesting way: Aaron and the tribe of Levi were "in the loins" of Abraham, yet unborn! So, when their father, Abraham, acknowledged the greatness of Melchizedek, the tribe of Levi was also involved. The Jewish people believe strongly in "racial solidarity," and this is one example of it. The paying of the tithes involved not just the patriarch Abraham, but also the unborn generations in his loins.

Since Jesus Christ came of "the seed of Abraham" (Heb. 2:16), does this mean that He, too, was a part of this experience? No, because Jesus Christ is the eternal Son of God. His identification with Abraham was for "the days of his flesh" (Heb. 5:7). Since Christ existed before Abraham (John 8:58), He could not have been "in Abraham" as were Aaron and his family.

2. THE DOCTRINAL ARGUMENT: CHRIST AND AARON (7:11–25)

In this section, the writer took his argument one step further. Not only is Melchizedek *greater than* Aaron, but Melchizedek has *replaced Aaron!* It is no longer the order of Aaron or the order of Levi. It is forever the order of Melchizedek. Why would God effect such a radical change?

Because both the priesthood and the law were imperfect (vv. 11–14). The words translated "perfect" and "perfection" are key words in this epistle (Heb. 2:10; 5:9; 6:1; 7:11, 19; 9:9; 10:1, 14). They essentially mean "completed, fulfilled." The Old Testament priests could not by their ministry complete the work of God in the heart of a worshipper. "For the law made nothing perfect" (Heb. 7:19). The animal sacrifices could not give any worshipper a perfect standing before God (Heb. 10:1–3). The Mosaic system of divine law was not a permanent system. It was "added" to serve as a "schoolmaster" to prepare the way for the coming of Christ (Gal. 3:19—4:7).

Since the priests received their authority from the Old Testament law (Heb. 7:28), and since the priesthood has been changed, there has also been a change in that law. The president of the United States cannot proclaim himself king of the United States because U.S. law makes no provision for a king. First, the law would have to be changed.

The law of Moses made no provision for a priesthood from the tribe of Judah (Heb. 7:14). Since our High Priest *is* from the tribe of Judah, according to His human ancestry, then there must have been a change in Moses' law. There has been! The entire system of Old Testament law has been fulfilled in Jesus Christ and has been taken out of the way (Col. 2:13–14). The believer has been set free from the law (Gal. 5:1–6) and is dead to the law (Rom. 7:1–4).

This new arrangement does not suggest that a Christian has the right to be lawless. "Free from the law" does not mean "free to sin." Rather, it means that we are free to do the will of God. We obey, not because of outward compulsion, but because of inward constraint (2 Cor. 5:14; Eph. 6:6). The indwelling Holy Spirit enables us to fulfill the "righteousness of the law" as we yield to Him (Rom. 8:1–4).

Because, being imperfect, the priesthood and the law could not continue forever (vv. 15–19). The word *another* in Hebrews 7:15 means "another of a different kind." The Levitical priests were made priests by the authority of a temporary and imperfect law. Jesus Christ was made Priest by a declaration of God. Because the law was "weak and useless" (Heb. 7:18 NIV), it could not continue forever. But because Jesus Christ is the eternal Son of God, He lives by "the power of an endless life" (Heb. 7:16). What a contrast between the profitless law and an endless life!

Since Jesus Christ is Priest *forever,* and since He has a nature to match that eternal priesthood, He can never be replaced. The annulling (Heb. 7:18, "disannulling") of the law meant the abolishing of the priesthood. But nobody can annul "the power of an endless life"! The logic holds: Jesus Christ is a Priest forever.

The writer kept in mind the temptation his readers were facing to go back into the old temple system. This is why he reminded them (Heb. 7:19) that Jesus Christ has accomplished what the law could never accomplish: He brought in a better hope, and He enables us to draw near to God. To go back to Judaism would mean losing the enjoyment of their fellowship with God through Christ. The only hope Judaism had was the coming of Christ, and that blessing these believers already had.

Because God's oath cannot be broken (vv. 20–22). No priest in the order of Aaron was ever ordained and established on the basis of God's personal oath. The Aaronic priests ministered "after the law of a carnal [physical] commandment" (Heb. 7:16). Their moral or spiritual fitness was not examined. The important thing was that a priest belonged to the right tribe and met the right physical and ceremonial requirements (Lev. 21:16–24).

Jesus Christ's heavenly priesthood was established on the basis of His work on the cross, His character (Heb. 2:10; 5:5–10), and the oath of God. "Thou art a priest for ever after the order of Melchizedek" (Heb. 7:21; Ps. 110:4). Note the introduction to the statement: "The Lord has sworn and will not change His mind" (NIV). The matter is finally settled and it cannot be changed.

The presence of this oath gives to the priesthood of our Lord a greater degree of permanence and assurance. Jesus Christ is the "surety of a better testament [covenant]" (Heb. 7:22). The word *surety* means "one who guarantees that the terms of an agreement will be carried out." Judah was willing to be the surety for Benjamin, to guarantee to their father that the boy would return home safely (Gen. 43:1–14). Paul was willing to be the surety for the slave Onesimus (Philem. 18–19). Perhaps the nearest equivalent we have today is a bondsman who posts bail for someone under indictment and guarantees that the indicted person will appear in court and stand trial.

As the Mediator between God and man (1 Tim. 2:5), Jesus Christ is God's great surety. Our risen and ever-living Savior guarantees that the terms of God's covenant will be fulfilled completely. God will not abandon

His people. But our Lord not only guarantees *to us* that God will fulfill the promises. As our Representative to God, He perfectly meets the terms of the agreement on our behalf. We of ourselves could never meet the terms, but because we have trusted Him, He has saved us and He has guaranteed that He will keep us.

In Hebrews 7:22, we have the first occurrence of a very important word in Hebrews—*testament*. This word, which is usually translated "covenant," is used twenty-one times in the letter, and it is the equivalent of "last will and testament." We will examine the word more closely in our study of Hebrews 8.

The writer has given three reasons why God changed the order of the priesthood from that of Aaron to that of Melchizedek: (1) The priesthood and the law were imperfect; (2) being imperfect, they could not continue forever; (3) God had sworn by His oath that the new order would be established. Then the writer of this letter to the Hebrews closed this section with a fourth reason.

Because, being men, the priests died (vv. 23–25). Not only was the priesthood imperfect, but it was also interrupted by death. There were *many* high priests because no one priest could live forever. In contrast, the church has *one* High Priest, Jesus the Son of God, who lives forever! An unchanging priest means an unchangeable priesthood, and this means security and confidence for God's people. "Jesus Christ the same yesterday, and to day, and for ever" (Heb. 13:8). "Thou art a priest for ever" (Ps. 110:4).

Occasionally we read a story in the newspaper about the illegal handling of a will. Perhaps some unscrupulous relative or business partner managed to get his hands on a will and use it for his own selfish purposes. But this could never happen to our Lord's "last will and testament" in His blood. He wrote the will and then died to make it take effect. But He arose from the dead and ascended to heaven, and there He is "probating" His own will!

The fact that the *unchanging* Christ continues as High Priest means, logically, that there is an "unchangeable priesthood" (Heb. 7:24). The Greek word translated "unchangeable" carries the idea of "valid and unalterable." The word was used at the end of legal contracts. Our Lord's priesthood in heaven is "valid and unalterable." Because it is, we can have confidence in the midst of this shaking, changing world.

What is the conclusion of the matter? It is stated in Hebrews 7:25: "Wherefore [because He is the ever-living, unchanging High Priest], he is able also to save them to the uttermost [completely, forever] that come unto God by him, seeing he ever liveth to make intercession for them." It is unfortunate that this verse is often read, "He is able to save *from* the uttermost" instead of "*to* the uttermost." To be sure, it is true that Christ can save any sinner from any condition; but that is not the import of the verse. The emphasis is on the fact that He saves completely, forever, all who put their faith in Him. Because He is our High Priest forever, He can save forever.

The basis for this completed salvation is the heavenly intercession of the Savior. The word translated "make intercession" simply means "to meet, to approach, to appeal, to make petition." We must not imagine that God the Father is angry with us so that God the Son must constantly appeal to Him not to judge us! The Father and the Son are in total agreement in the plan of salvation (Heb. 13:20–21). Neither should we imagine our Lord Jesus uttering prayers on our behalf in heaven, or repeatedly "offering His blood" as a sacrifice. That work was completed on the cross once and for all.

Intercession involves our Lord's representation of His people at the throne of God. Through Christ, believers are able to draw near to God in prayer and also to offer spiritual sacrifices to God (Heb. 4:14–16; 1 Peter 2:5). It has well been said that Christ's life in heaven is His prayer for us. It is what He *is* that determines what He *does*.

In reviewing the reasoning found in this long section (Heb. 7:11–25), we are impressed with the logic of the writer. Jesus Christ's priesthood after the order of Melchizedek is superior to that of Aaron and has replaced it. Both the historical argument and the doctrinal argument are sound. But the writer adds a third argument.

3. THE PRACTICAL ARGUMENT: CHRIST AND THE BELIEVER (7:26–28)

No matter how devoted and obedient the Aaronic priests were, they could not always meet the needs of all the people. But Jesus Christ perfectly meets all of our needs. "For such an high priest became us" means "He was suited to us; He meets our needs completely." The emphasis here is on His sinlessness. Being perfect, He is able to exercise a perfect ministry for His people. Because of their sins, some of the Old Testament priests not only were unable to serve the people, but actually abused them. This could never happen with Jesus Christ and His people.

The Old Testament priests were "set apart" for their ministry, so in that sense they were "holy." But they were not always holy in character. They were sinners like the people to whom they ministered. "Harmless" (Heb. 7:26) means "blameless." No Jewish priest could claim this distinction. "Undefiled" means "unstained." Again, only Jesus Christ can claim these characteristics. When He was ministering on earth, our Lord was a friend of publicans and sinners (Matt. 9:10; 11:19), but His contact with them did not defile His character or His conduct. There was contact without contamination. He was not isolated; He was separated. Today, He is "separate from sinners" because of His position ("made higher than the heavens"), but He is not separated from the people to whom He ministers. He is always available to us at His throne of grace.

Another proof of His sinlessness is the fact that our Lord never had to offer sacrifices for His own cleansing, as did the priests. On the *annual* Day of Atonement, the high priest first had to sacrifice for himself before he could sacrifice for the people (Lev. 16). There were also *daily* sacrifices offered as a part of the temple ritual, and, if a priest had sinned, he had to bring a sacrifice for his own cleansing (Ex. 29:38–46; Lev. 4:3ff.). But Jesus Christ offered just one sacrifice for our sins and settled the matter forever (see Heb. 9:23–28).

This is the kind of High Priest we need! We are prone to sin daily, even hourly, and we need to be able to turn to Him for spiritual help. As our High Priest, Jesus Christ gives us the grace and mercy that *we need not sin.* But if we do sin, He is our Advocate at God's throne (1 John 2:1–2). If we confess our sins to Him, He forgives us and restores us (1 John 1:9).

The application is obvious: Why turn away from such an adequate High Priest? What more can you find in any other person? The men who served under the law of Moses had human infirmities and weaknesses, and they often failed. Our heavenly High Priest has been "consecrated [perfected] for evermore" (Heb. 7:28) and there is no spot or blemish in Him. Such a High Priest "suits us perfectly"!

Are you availing yourself of His gracious ministry?

QUESTIONS FOR PERSONAL REFLECTION
OR GROUP DISCUSSION

1. Read Genesis 14:17–20 and Psalm 110:4–5. What picture do you get of Melchizedek from these verses?

2. In your own life, how have you seen a parallel between righteousness and peace?

3. What is your theory as to why civilizations were already offering a tithe to God before the commandment to tithe was given to Moses?

4. The Levites were priests because of their blood line, not their character. What problems could that have posed for the temple?

5. Why do you think Christ "set aside" the law (Heb. 7:18 NIV)? Did the law stop being necessary?

6. If we are not constrained by the Old Testament law of God in our behavior, what are we constrained by? How does that work in practice?

7. Describe the security we have in the fact that Jesus will never die.

8. What are the differences between the old covenant that Jesus set aside and this "better covenant" that He became surety for?

9. If we begin living our lives more aware of the reality that we have Christ on our side, speaking to God on our behalf, what might be some of the ways our lives will change?

Chapter Seven

THE BETTER COVENANT

(Hebrews 8)

I once spoke at a meeting of religious broadcasters at which a friend of mine was to provide the ministry of music. He is a superb pianist with a gift for interpreting Christian music, and I have always enjoyed listening to him. But that day my heart went out to him in sympathy, because the motel had provided the most deteriorated and derelict piano I have ever seen. It must have been donated by a local wrecking company. My friend did his best, but it would have been much better had he been playing a decent instrument.

Jesus Christ is God's superior Priest, but is there anything that can minimize this superiority? Nothing! For He ministers on the basis of a better covenant (Heb. 8), in a better sanctuary (Heb. 9), and because of a better sacrifice (Heb. 10). It is the better covenant that is the theme of this chapter. The writer presented three evidences for the superiority of this covenant.

1. IT IS MINISTERED BY A SUPERIOR HIGH PRIEST (8:1–2)

Was the writer arguing in circles? First he showed the superiority of Christ, and then said, "Since He is superior, the covenant He ministers must be a superior covenant." No, this is not reasoning in a circle, for the conclusion is logical. A superior priest could never minister on the basis of an inferior covenant. To change the illustration, the most gifted lawyer can do very little if the will he is probating is inadequate. It is unthinkable that our Lord would minister on the basis of an inferior "last will and testament."

"This is the sum" simply means "this is the main point and the climax of my discussion." He then presented several summary arguments to prove that our Lord is indeed a superior High Priest.

His moral adequacy (v. 1). "We have *such* an High Priest." This statement refers us back to Hebrews 7:22–28. "For *such an high priest* became us [was suited to us]" (Heb. 7:26). The fact that Jesus Christ is morally perfect and yet identified with us in our needs and temptations makes Him superior to any other priest, past or present. Those readers who wanted to go back into the Old Testament priesthood would have to leave this *suitable* High Priest.

His finished work (v. 1). Today our Lord is *seated* because His work is complete. There were no chairs in the Old Testament tabernacle because the work of the priests was never finished. Each repeated sacrifice was only a reminder that *none* of the sacrifices ever provided a finished salvation. The blood of animals did not wash away sin or cleanse the guilty conscience; it only covered sin until that day when Jesus Christ died to take away the sin of the world (John 1:29).

His enthronement (v. 1). Jesus Christ is not just "seated." It is *where* He is seated that adds glory to His person and His work. He is seated on the throne in heaven at the right hand of the Father. This great truth was introduced early in this epistle (Heb. 1:3), and it will be mentioned again (Heb. 10:12; 12:2). This enthronement was the fulfillment of the Father's promise to the Son: "Sit thou at my right hand, until I make thine enemies thy footstool" (Ps. 110:1). Not only did the high priest of Israel never sit down in the tabernacle, but he never sat down *on a throne.* Only a priest "after the order of Melchizedek" could be enthroned, for Melchizedek was both king and priest (Heb. 7:1).

His supreme exaltation (vv. 1–2). He is "in the heavens." Jesus Christ, in His ascension and exaltation, "passed through the heavens" (Heb. 4:14 NASB). He is now exalted as high as anyone could be (Eph. 1:20–23; Phil. 2:5–11). The fact that He ministers in a *heavenly* sanctuary is important to the argument presented in this chapter.

As we review these four summary arguments, we can see how logical it is that our Lord ministers on the basis of a superior covenant. Can you conceive of a high priest who is perfect morally, ministering on the basis of a covenant that could not change human hearts? Could a priest who has *finished* his work minister from a covenant that could finish nothing? Can we conceive of a king-priest in the highest heaven being limited by an old covenant that made nothing perfect (Heb. 7:19)? The conclusion seems reasonable: The presence of a superior High Priest in heaven demands a superior covenant if He is to minister effectively to God's people.

2. It Is Ministered in a Better Place (8:3–5)

In this paragraph, the writer expanded on the marvelous truth that Jesus Christ today ministers in the heavenly sanctuary. The reason for this discussion is not difficult to determine. His readers knew that there was a real temple in Jerusalem, and that in the temple there were priests offering gifts and sacrifices. How easy it would be to go back into the traditional Mosaic system! After all, how do we *know* that the Lord Jesus is ministering in a sanctuary? Has anyone actually seen Him in His high-priestly work?

Good questions—and there are good answers!

The logical answer (v. 3). It has already been determined that Jesus Christ is a high priest. But all high priests serve others; the title is not honorary. Each Old Testament high priest was appointed "to offer gifts and sacrifices"; therefore, Jesus Christ must offer gifts and sacrifices (see Heb. 5:1; 7:27). But these sacrifices must not be offered just anywhere; they must be offered in God's appointed place (Deut. 12:13–14). That appointed place is the sanctuary. The conclusion is logical: If Jesus Christ is a High Priest who offers gifts and sacrifices, then He must have a sanctuary in which He ministers. Since He is in heaven, that sanctuary must be in heaven.

We must not, however, get the impression that our Lord is offering sacrifices in heaven that correspond to the Old Testament sacrifices. The word *somewhat* in Hebrews 8:3 is in the singular, and the phrase *to offer* is in a Greek tense that implies "offer once and for all." On the cross, He offered Himself as the one sacrifice for sin forever (Heb. 9:24–28). In other words, our Lord is "a living sacrifice" in heaven. He is not offering Himself over and over because that is unnecessary.

The genealogical answer (v. 4). We have met this truth before in Hebrews 7:11–14. As far as His human ancestry is concerned, our Lord came from the tribe of Judah. God had promised that the Messiah would come from the kingly tribe of Judah (Gen. 49:8–10). But the priests had to come from the tribe of Levi. Therefore, if Jesus Christ were still on earth, He could not function as a priest. But He can serve as High Priest in heaven because there the order of Melchizedek governs the ministry, not the order of Aaron.

Again, the argument is sound. David predicted that Jesus Christ would be a Priest (Ps. 110:4). Jesus' earthly birth into the tribe of Judah would not permit Him to be an earthly priest; therefore, He must be a Priest in heaven. He would not be accepted in the earthly sanctuary, so He must be serving in the heavenly sanctuary.

The typological answer (v. 5). A "type" is an Old Testament picture of a New Testament truth. Each type is identified as such in the New Testament, so we must not try to make every Old Testament person or event into a type. The word *pattern* in this verse is the Greek word *tupos,* from which we get our English word *type*.

The priests then serving in the temple were actually serving in a sanctuary that was a copy ("example") of the heavenly sanctuary. The quotation is from Exodus 25:40, where it refers obliquely to a heavenly sanctuary. Moses saw this pattern on the mount and duplicated its essentials in the earthly tabernacle. This does not mean that the heavenly tabernacle is made up of skins and fabrics. It is the basic pattern and meaning of the sanctuary that is emphasized here. The true sanctuary is in heaven; the tabernacle and temple were but imitations or copies of the true.

This is a telling argument for remaining faithful to Jesus Christ and not going back into Judaism. The earthly priesthood and sanctuary seemed quite real and stable, and yet they were but *copies* of the true! The Old Testament system was but shadows (see Col. 2:17). The law was but a "shadow of good things to come" (Heb. 10:1); the true and full light came in Jesus Christ. So why go back into the shadows?

In the book of Revelation, where the heavenly scene is described, we can find parallels to the Old Testament tabernacle. John stated that there is a temple of God in heaven (Rev. 11:19). Of course, there will be no temple in the eternal state, because the entire city of God will be a temple (Rev. 21:22). For example, there is a brazen altar (Rev. 6:9–11), as well as an altar of incense (Rev. 8:3–5). The "sea of glass" (Rev. 4:6) reminds us of the laver, and the seven lamps of fire (Rev. 4:5) suggest the seven-branched lampstand in the tabernacle.

Since Jesus Christ is ministering in the original sanctuary, and not the copy, He is ministering in a better place. Why fellowship with priests who are serving in a *copied* sanctuary when you can fellowship with Christ in the original heavenly sanctuary? It would be like trying to live on the blueprint instead of in the building itself!

The writer has now given us two evidences of the superiority of the new covenant: It is ministered by a superior Priest, Jesus Christ; and it is ministered in a superior place, heaven itself. He devoted the remainder of this section to the third evidence.

3. IT IS FOUNDED ON BETTER PROMISES (8:6–13)

Moses was the mediator (go-between) of the old covenant in the giving of the law (Gal. 3:19–20). The people of Israel were so frightened at Mount Sinai that they begged Moses to speak to them so that they would not have to hear God speak (Ex. 20:18–21). Sad to say, this fear of God did not last long, for the people soon disobeyed the very law they promised to keep. The Mediator of the new covenant is Jesus Christ, and He is the only Mediator (1 Tim. 2:5). Christ's ministry as Mediator is more excellent than that of the Old Testament priests because it is based on a better covenant; *and His covenant is founded on better promises.*

The "better covenant" that is referred to in this paragraph was announced by the prophet Jeremiah (Jer. 31:31–34). The promise was given in a prophecy that assured the Jews of future restoration. Jeremiah ministered during the closing years of the nation's history, before Judah went into Babylonian captivity. At a time when the nation's future seemed completely destroyed, God gave the promise of restoration and blessing.

Before our Lord went to Calvary, He celebrated the Passover with His disciples in the upper room. At that supper, He instituted what we call "the Lord's Supper." He said, taking the cup, "This cup is the new testament [covenant] in my blood, which is shed for you" (Luke 22:20). The apostle Paul quoted these words and applied them to the church (1 Cor. 11:23–27). The writer of Hebrews states clearly that Jesus Christ *now* "is the mediator of the new testament" (Heb. 9:15) and repeats it (Heb. 12:24).

What, then, is the relationship between this new covenant *promised* to Israel, but today *experienced* by the church? Or, to state it another way, how can God promise these blessings to the Jews and then turn around and give them to the church?

Some Bible students solve the problem by concluding that the church is "spiritual Israel" and that the new covenant promises therefore belong to "Abraham's spiritual seed" today. That believers today are the "spiritual seed" of Abraham is clear from Galatians 3:13–29; but this is not the same as saying that the church is "spiritual Israel." The promise quoted in Hebrews 8:8 specifically names "the house of Israel and … the house of Judah." Once we are permitted to make such plain words as "Israel" and "Judah" mean something else, there is no end to how we might interpret the Bible!

Other students believe that this "new covenant" has no present fulfillment in the church, but that it will be fulfilled only when the Jews are regathered and the kingdom is established at our Lord's return to earth in glory. But then we have the problem of explaining Hebrews 9:15 and 12:24, verses that state that Jesus Christ is *today* the Mediator of the new covenant. To affirm that there are *two* "new covenants," one for Israel and one for the church, is to create more questions!

Perhaps the solution is found in God's principle of "to the Jew first" (Rom. 1:16). God did promise a new covenant for His people, but the blessings of this covenant are wrapped up in God's Son, Jesus Christ. He is the Mediator of the new covenant. When Jesus began His ministry on earth, He went to His own people first (Matt. 15:24). When He sent out His disciples, He sent them only to Israel (Matt. 10:5–6). When He commissioned the church to witness, He instructed them to begin in Jerusalem (Luke 24:46–48; Acts 1:8). Peter's message at Pentecost was addressed only to Jews and to Gentiles who were Jewish proselytes (see Acts 2:14, 22, 36).

In his second recorded sermon, Peter clearly stated that the good news of the gospel would go to the Jews first (Acts 3:25–26).

But the nation rejected the message and the messengers. While it is true that thousands of individuals trusted Christ and were saved, it is also true that most of the nation rejected the Word, and that the religious leaders opposed the ministry of the church. One result was the stoning of Stephen (Acts 7). But what was God's response? The gospel moved from Jerusalem and Judea into Samaria (Acts 8), and then to the Gentiles (Acts 10).

The church today is made up of regenerated Jews and Gentiles who are one body in Christ (Eph. 2:11–22; Gal. 3:27–29). All who are "in Christ" share in the new covenant, which was purchased on the cross. Today the blessings of the new covenant are applied to individuals. When Jesus comes in glory to redeem Israel, then the blessings of the new covenant will be applied to that beleaguered nation. Read all of Jeremiah 31 to see what God has planned for Israel, His people.

Before we examine the "better promises" of the new covenant, we must settle another matter. We must not conclude that the existence of the new covenant means that the old covenant was wrong or that the law has no ministry today. Both covenants were given by God. Both covenants were given for people's good. Both covenants had blessings attached to them. If Israel had obeyed the terms of the old covenant, God would have blessed them and they would have been ready for the coming of their Messiah. Paul pointed out that the old covenant had its share of glory (2 Cor. 3:7–11). We must not criticize the old covenant or minimize it.

Even though the new covenant of grace brings with it freedom from the law of Moses (Gal. 5:1), it does not bring freedom to disobey God and to sin. God still desires that the "righteousness of the law" should be fulfilled in us through the ministry of the Holy Spirit (Rom. 8:1–4). There is a lawful use of the law (1 Tim. 1:8–11).

Now we are ready to consider the "better promises" that belong to the new covenant.

The promise of God's grace (vv. 7–9). The emphasis in the new covenant is on God's "I will." The nation of Israel at Sinai said, "All the words which the Lord hath said will we do" (Ex. 24:3). But they did not obey God's words. It is one thing to *say* "We will!" and quite another thing to do it. But the new covenant does not depend on man's faithfulness to God but on God's faithful promise to man. The writer of Hebrews affirmed God's "I will" on behalf of those who trust Jesus Christ (Heb. 8:10). In fact, God's "I will" is stated three times in that one verse and six times in Hebrews 8:8–12.

God led Israel out of Egypt the way a father would take a child by the hand and lead him. God gave Israel His holy law for their own good, to separate them from the other nations and to protect them from the sinful practices of the heathen. But the nation failed; "they continued not in my covenant" (Heb. 8:9). God's responses to Israel's disobedience were to discipline them repeatedly and finally to send them into captivity.

God did not find fault with His covenant but with His people. "Wherefore the law is holy, and the commandment holy, and just, and good" (Rom. 7:12). The problem is not with the law, but with our sinful natures, for by ourselves we cannot keep God's law. The law "made nothing perfect" (Heb. 7:19) because it could not change any human heart. Only God's grace can do that.

The new covenant is *wholly* of God's grace; no sinner can become a part of this new covenant without faith in Jesus Christ. Grace and faith go together just as the law and works go together (Rom. 11:6). The law says, "The man that doeth them [the things written in the law] shall live in them" (Gal. 3:12). But grace says, "The work is done—believe and live!"

The promise of internal change (v. 10). The law of Moses could *declare*

God's holy standard, but it could never *provide* the power needed for obedience. Sinful people need a new heart and a new disposition within; and this is just what the new covenant provides. (For a parallel passage, see Ezek. 36:26–27.) When a sinner trusts Christ, he receives a divine nature within (2 Peter 1:1–4). This divine nature creates a desire to love and obey God. By nature, sinful people are hateful and disobedient (Titus 3:3–7), but the new nature gives each believer both the desire and the dynamic for a godly life.

The law was external; God's demands were written on tablets of stone. But the new covenant makes it possible for God's Word to be written on human minds and hearts (2 Cor. 3:1–3). God's grace makes possible an internal transformation that makes a surrendered believer more and more like Jesus Christ (2 Cor. 3:18).

It is unfortunate that many Christians think they are saved by grace but must then fulfill their Christian life according to the Old Testament law. They want the new covenant for salvation but the old covenant for sanctification. The apostle Paul had a phrase to describe this condition: "fallen from grace" (Gal. 5:4). Not "fallen from salvation," but fallen from the sphere of God's blessing through grace. We do not become holy people by trying to obey God's law in our own power. It is by yielding to the Holy Spirit within that we fulfill the righteousness of the law (Rom. 8:1–4); and this is wholly of grace.

The promise of forgiveness for all (vv. 11–12). There is no forgiveness under the law because the law was not given for that purpose. "Therefore by the deeds of the law there shall no flesh be justified in his sight; for by the law is the knowledge of sin" (Rom. 3:20). The law could not promise forgiveness to Israel, let alone to all mankind. It is only through the sacrifice of Jesus Christ that forgiveness is possible to all who will call on Him. The Old Testament sacrifices brought a *remembrance* of sins, not a *remission* of sins (Heb. 10:1–3, 18).

Hebrews 8:11 quotes Jeremiah 31:34. It refers to that day when Israel shall be reunited with Judah (Heb. 8:8) and shall rejoice in the promised kingdom (Jer. 31:1–14). In that day, there will be no need to share the gospel with others because everyone will know the Lord personally. However, until that day, it is both our privilege and our responsibility to share the gospel message with a lost world.

What does it mean that God remembers our sins and iniquities no more (Heb. 8:12)? This important statement is quoted again in Hebrews 10:16–17. Does it mean that our all-knowing God can actually *forget* what we have done? If God forgot anything, He would cease to be God! The phrase "remember no more" means "hold against us no more." God recalls what we have done, but He does not hold it against us. He deals with us on the basis of grace and mercy, not law and merit. Once sin has been forgiven, it is never brought before us again. The matter is settled eternally.

As a pastor in counseling ministry I have often heard people say, "Well, I can forgive—but I cannot forget!"

"Of course you can't forget," I usually reply. "The more you try to put this thing out of your mind, the more you will remember it. But that isn't what it means to forget." Then I go on to explain that "to forget" means "not to hold it against the person who has wronged us." We may remember what others have done, but we treat them *as though they never did it.*

How is this possible? It is possible because of the cross, for there God treated His Son *as though He had done it!* Our experience of forgiveness from God makes it possible for us to forgive others.

The promise of eternal blessing (v. 13). The old covenant was still governing the nation of Israel at the time this epistle was written. The temple was standing and the priests were offering their appointed sacrifices.

Devout Jews probably thought that their Christian friends were foolish to abandon such a "solid religion" for a faith that was seemingly intangible. What the unbelieving Jews did not realize was that their "solid religion" had grown old and was about to vanish away. In AD 70 the city of Jerusalem and the temple were destroyed by the Romans, and the Jews have not had a temple or a priesthood to serve them ever since (see Hos. 3:4).

However, the new covenant brings eternal blessing. Jesus Christ is the Author of "eternal salvation" (Heb. 5:9) and "eternal redemption" (Heb. 9:12). The new covenant can never get old and disappear. The Greek word translated "new" means "new in quality," not "new in time." This new covenant is of such quality that it will never need to be replaced!

Yes, our Lord is ministering on the basis of a better covenant, a new covenant that makes us partakers of the new nature and the wonderful new life that only Christ can give.

QUESTIONS FOR PERSONAL REFLECTION
OR GROUP DISCUSSION

1. Describe the traits and lifestyle of a person who is morally pure.

2. Christ is seated in heaven because His work in redeeming us is complete. What about our part of accepting His redemption? What do we do to complete our part of the work in our own lives?

3. What covenant do you, as a believer, have with God? What have each of you already done to establish this covenant? What have each of you agreed to do now and in the future?

4. Describe some of the differences between the old covenant and the new covenant.

5. Under the new covenant, God puts His law in our minds and writes it on our hearts (Heb. 8:10). Have you experienced this? If so, give an example of how.

6. How does the presence of God's grace through Christ make our covenant radically different from the old one?

7. Give an example of a time when God gave you grace.

8. Read Matthew 5:27–32. What was Christ telling His listeners about the new covenant in terms of exterior and interior evidences?

9. How is the way you experience God's love and forgiveness under the new covenant far different from the way an Old Testament Israelite would have experienced God's love and forgiveness under the old covenant?

10. Why will this new covenant never need to be overhauled or replaced?

THE SUPERIOR SANCTUARY

(Hebrews 9)

The Christian is a citizen of two worlds, the earthly and the heavenly. He must render to Caesar the things that are Caesar's and to God the things that are God's (Matt. 22:21). Because he is a citizen of two worlds, he must learn how to walk by faith in a world that is governed by sight. Like Moses, a believer must see the invisible if he is to overcome the pull of the world (Heb. 11:24–27). Practical man says, "Seeing is believing!" But the man of faith replies, "Believing is seeing!"

This principle of faith must apply to our relationship to the heavenly sanctuary. We have never seen this sanctuary. Yet we believe what the Bible tells us about it. We realize that God is not worshipped today in temples made with hands (Acts 7:46–50). There is no special place on earth where God dwells (see Isa. 57:15; 66:1–2; John 4:19–24). We may call a local church building a "house of God," but we know that God does not live there. The building is dedicated to God and His service, but it is not His dwelling place.

Hebrews 9 presents a detailed contrast between the old covenant sanctuary (the tabernacle) and the new covenant heavenly sanctuary where Jesus Christ now ministers. This contrast makes it clear that the new covenant sanctuary is superior.

THE INFERIOR OLD COVENANT SANCTUARY (9:1–10)

Hebrews reminds readers that the regulations and practices in the tabernacle were ordained of God. If there was any inferiority in the tabernacle service, it was not because God had not established the ritual. While the old covenant was in force, the ministry of the priests was ordained of God and perfectly proper.

What was it, then, that made the tabernacle inferior? There are five answers to that question.

(1) It was an earthly sanctuary (v. 1). This means it was made by man (Heb. 9:11) and pitched by man (Heb. 8:2). The Jewish people generously brought their gifts to Moses, and from these materials the tabernacle was constructed. Then God gave spiritual wisdom and skill to Bezaleel and Oholiab to do the intricate work of making the various parts of the tabernacle and its furnishings (see Ex. 35—36). After the construction was completed, the sanctuary was put in place and dedicated to God (Ex. 40). Even though the glory of God moved into the sanctuary, it was still an earthly building, constructed by humans out of earthly materials.

Being an earthly building, it had several weaknesses. For one thing, it would need a certain amount of repair. Also, it was limited geographically: If it was pitched in one place, it could not be in another place. It had to be dismantled and the various parts carried from place to place. Furthermore, it belonged to the nation of Israel and not to the whole world.

(2) It was a type of something greater (vv. 2–5). The writer listed the various parts and furnishings of the tabernacle because each of these carried a spiritual meaning. They were "patterns of things in the heavens" (Heb. 9:23). The following diagram gives a general picture of the tabernacle.

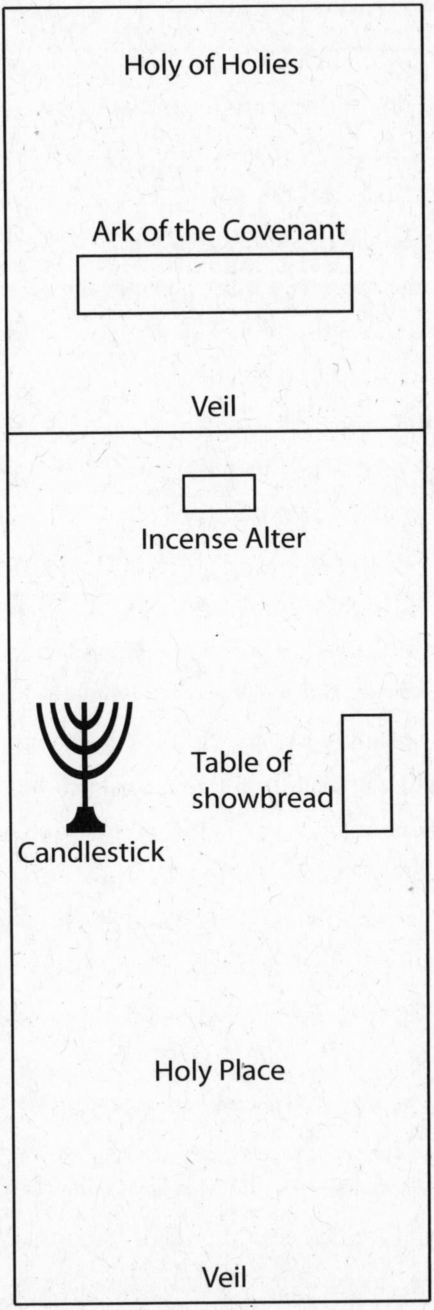

Holy of Holies

Ark of the Covenant

Veil

Incense Alter

Candlestick

Table of
showbread

Holy Place

Veil

The phrases "the first" (Heb. 9:2) and "the second" (Heb. 9:7) refer to the first and second divisions of the tabernacle. The first was called the Holy Place and the second the Holy of Holies. Each of these divisions had its own furnishings, and each piece of furniture had its own special meaning.

In the Holy Place stood the seven-branched golden candlestick (Ex. 25:31–40; 27:20–21; 37:17–24). "Lampstand" would be a better term to use, because the light was produced by the burning of wicks in oil, not by the use of candles. Since there were no windows in the tabernacle, this lampstand provided the necessary light for the priests' ministry in the Holy Place. The nation of Israel was supposed to be a light to the nations (Isa. 42:6; 49:6). Jesus Christ is the "light of the world" (John 8:12), and believers are to shine as lights in the world (Phil. 2:14–15).

There was also a table in the Holy Place with twelve loaves of bread on it. It was called the Table of Showbread (Ex. 25:23–30; 37:10–16; Lev. 24:5–9). Each Sabbath, the priests would remove the old loaves and put fresh loaves on the table, and the old loaves would be eaten. These loaves were called "the bread of presence." Only the priests could eat this bread, and they were required to eat it in the sanctuary. It reminded the twelve tribes of God's presence that sustained them. It also speaks to us today of Jesus Christ, the "bread of life" given to the whole world (John 6).

The golden altar stood in the Holy Place just in front of the veil that divided the two parts of the tabernacle. The word translated "censer" (a device for burning incense) (Heb. 9:4) should be "altar." The golden altar did not stand in the Holy of Holies, but its ministry *pertained* to the Holy of Holies. In what way? On the annual Day of Atonement, the high priest used coals from this altar to burn incense before the mercy seat within the veil (Lev. 16:12–14). Moses (Ex. 40:5) related the golden altar to the ark of the covenant, and so did the author of 1 Kings (1 Kings 6:22). Each morning and evening, a priest burned incense on this altar. David suggested that it is a picture of prayer ascending to God (Ps. 141:2). It can be a reminder that Jesus Christ intercedes for us (Rom. 8:33–34). (For details about this incense altar, see Exodus 30:1–10; 37:25–29. The incense itself is described in Exodus 30:34–35.)

The Holy of Holies contained only the ark of the covenant, a wooden chest three feet, nine inches long; two feet, three inches wide; and two feet, three inches high. On the top of this chest was a beautiful "mercy seat" made of gold, with a cherub at each end. This was the throne of God in the tabernacle (Ex. 25:10–22; Ps. 80:1; 99:1). On the Day of Atonement, the blood was sprinkled on this mercy seat to cover the tables of law within the ark. God did not look at the broken law; He saw the blood. Christ is our "mercy seat" ("propitiation" in 1 John 2:2; Rom. 3:25). But His blood does not just cover sin; it takes away sin.

No doubt many spiritual truths are wrapped up in these pieces of furniture, and all of them are of value. But the most important truth is this: All of this was *symbolism* and not the spiritual *reality*. It was this fact that made the tabernacle of the old covenant inferior.

(3) It was inaccessible to the people (vv. 6–7). We must not get the idea that the Jews assembled in the tabernacle for worship. The priests and Levites were permitted into the tabernacle precincts, but not the people from the other tribes. Furthermore, though the priests ministered in the Holy Place day after day, only the high priest entered the Holy of Holies, and that only once a year. When he did, he had to offer a sacrifice for his own sins as well as for the sins of the people. In contrast, the heavenly tabernacle is open to all of the people of God, and at all times (Heb. 10:19–25)!

(4) It was temporary (v. 8). The fact that the outer court ("first tabernacle," Heb. 9:6) was standing was proof that God's work of salvation for man had not yet been completed. The outer court stood between the people and the Holy of Holies! As long as the priests were ministering in the

Holy Place, the way had not yet been opened into the presence of God. But when Jesus died on the cross, the veil of the temple was torn from top to bottom (Matt. 27:50–51) and the way was opened into the Holy of Holies. There was no longer any more need for either the Holy Place or the Holy of Holies, for now believing sinners could come into the presence of God.

(5) Its ministry was external, not internal (vv. 9–10). The sacrifices offered and the blood applied to the mercy seat could never change the heart or the conscience of a worshipper. All of the ceremonies associated with the tabernacle had to do with ceremonial purity, not moral purity. They were "carnal ordinances" that pertained to the outer man but that could not change the inner man.

THE SUPERIOR HEAVENLY SANCTUARY (9:11–28)

The five deficiencies of the old covenant sanctuary are matched with the five superiorities of the new covenant sanctuary. In every way, the present sanctuary is superior.

(1) It is heavenly (v. 11). The writer has emphasized this fact before, because he has wanted his readers to focus their attention on the things of heaven and not on the things of earth. Some things on earth (including the beautiful Jewish temple) would soon be destroyed; but the heavenly realities would endure forever.

The old covenant tabernacle was made by the hands of men (Ex. 35:30–35). The new covenant sanctuary was not made with hands. "Not of this building" (Heb. 9:11) means "not of this creation." The tabernacle of Moses was made with materials that belong to this creation. The heavenly tabernacle needed no such materials (Heb. 9:24). Since the heavenly tabernacle does not belong to this creation, it is free from the ravages of time.

The "good things to come" had already arrived! All that was foreshadowed by type in the tabernacle was now reality because of Christ's priestly ministry in heaven. The tabernacle was patterned after the sanctuary in heaven, but today we no longer need the pattern. We have the eternal reality!

(2) Its ministry is effective to deal with sin (vv. 12–15). We have here a series of contrasts that show again the superiority of the heavenly ministry.

Animal sacrifices and Christ's sacrifice (v. 12). The writer will discuss the inferiority of animal sacrifices in Hebrews 10, but here he began to lay the foundation. We need no proof that the blood of Jesus Christ is far superior to that of animal sacrifices. How can the blood of *animals* ever solve the problem of *humans'* sins? Jesus Christ became a man that He might be able to die for people's sins. His death was voluntary; it is doubtful that any Old Testament sacrifice volunteered for the job! An animal's blood was carried by the high priest into the Holy of Holies, but Jesus Christ presented *Himself* in the presence of God as the final and complete sacrifice for sins. Of course, the animal sacrifices were repeated, while Jesus Christ offered Himself but once. Finally, no animal sacrifices ever purchased "eternal redemption." Their blood could only "cover" sin until the time when Christ's blood would "taketh away sin" (John 1:29). We have "eternal redemption." It is not conditioned on our merit or good works; it is secured once and for all by the finished work of Jesus Christ.

Ceremonial cleansing and conscience cleansing (vv. 13–14). The old covenant rituals could not change a person's heart. This is not to say that a worshipper did not have a spiritual experience if his heart trusted God, but it does mean that the emphasis was on the external ceremonial cleansing. So long as the worshipper obeyed the prescribed regulations, he was declared clean. It was "the purifying of the flesh" but not the cleansing of the conscience. (For "the ashes of the heifer," see Num. 19.)

We learned from Hebrews 8 that the ministry of the new covenant is *internal.* "I will put my laws into their mind, and write them in their hearts" (Heb. 8:10). This work is done by the Holy Spirit of God (2 Cor. 3:1–3). But the Spirit could not dwell within us if Jesus Christ had not paid for our sins. Cleansing our consciences cannot be done by some external ceremony; it demands an internal power. Because Jesus Christ is "without spot [blemish]" He was able to offer the perfect sacrifice.

Temporary blessings and eternal blessings (v. 15). The blessings under the old covenant depended on the obedience of God's people. If they obeyed God, He blessed them, but if they disobeyed, He withheld His blessings. Not only were the blessings temporary, but they were primarily *temporal—* rain, bumper crops, protection from enemies and sickness, and so forth. Israel's Canaan inheritance involved material blessings. Our eternal inheritance is primarily spiritual in nature (Eph. 1:3). Note that the emphasis is on *eternal—*"eternal redemption" (Heb. 9:12) and "eternal inheritance" (Heb. 9:15). A believer can have confidence because all that he has in Christ is eternal.

This verse (Heb. 9:15) makes it clear that there was no final and complete redemption under the old covenant. Those transgressions were *covered* by the blood of the many sacrifices, but not *cleansed* until the sacrifice of Jesus Christ on the cross (Rom. 3:24–26). Since Christ has accomplished an eternal redemption, we are able to share in an eternal inheritance.

As we review these three contrasts, we can easily see that the ministry of Christ is effective to deal with our sins. His finished work on earth, and His unfinished work of intercession in heaven are sufficient and efficient.

(3) Its ministry is based on a costly sacrifice (vv. 16–23). The word covenant not only means "an agreement," but it also carries the idea of "a last will and testament." If a man writes his will, that will is not in force until he dies. It was necessary for Jesus Christ to die so that the terms of the new covenant might be enforced. "This cup is the new testament [covenant, will] in my blood, which is shed for you" (Luke 22:20).

Even the old covenant was established on the basis of blood. Hebrews 9:19–21 is taken from Exodus 24:3–8, the account of the ratifying of the old covenant by Moses and the people of Israel. The book of the law was sprinkled with blood, and so were the people and the tabernacle and its furnishings. It must have been a solemn occasion.

Not only was blood used at the *beginning* of the ministry of the old covenant, but it was used in the *regular* administration of the tabernacle service. Under the old covenant, people and objects were purified by blood, water, or fire (Num. 31:21–24). This was, of course, *ceremonial* purification; it meant that the persons and objects were now acceptable to God. The purification did not alter the nature of the person or object. God's principle is that blood must be shed before sin can be forgiven (Lev. 17:11).

Since God has ordained that remission of sins is through the *shedding* of blood, and since purification comes through the *sprinkling* of blood, it is necessary that blood be shed and applied if the new covenant is to be in force. The "patterns" (the old covenant tabernacle) were purified by the sprinkling of the blood. But the "originals" were also purified! The blood of Jesus Christ not only purifies the conscience of the believer (Heb. 9:14), but also purified the "heavenly things" (Heb. 9:23 NASB).

How could the heavenly sanctuary ever become defiled? We can understand how the *earthly* sanctuary could be defiled since it was used by sinful men. Each year, on the great Day of Atonement, the tabernacle was purified through the sprinkling of blood (Lev. 16:12–19). But how could a heavenly sanctuary ever become defiled? Certainly nothing in heaven is defiled in a literal sense, for sin cannot pollute the sanctuary of God. But, for that matter, nothing in the earthly tabernacle was *literally* defiled by sin.

It all had to do with people's relationships to God. The blood sprinkled on a piece of furniture did not change the nature of that piece, *but it changed God's relationship to it.* God could enter into communion with people because of the sprinkled blood.

Through Jesus Christ, we who are sinners can enter into the Holy of Holies in the heavenly sanctuary (Heb. 10:19–22). Physically, of course, we are on earth, but spiritually, we are communing with God in the heavenly Holy of Holies. In order for God to receive us into this heavenly fellowship, the blood of Jesus Christ *had to be applied.* We enter into God's presence "by the blood of Jesus" (Heb. 10:19).

Now we can summarize the writer's discussion. The old covenant was established by blood, and so was the new covenant. But the new covenant was established on the basis of a better sacrifice, applied in a better place! The patterns (types) were purified by the blood of animals, but the original sanctuary was purified by the blood of the Son of God. This was a far more costly sacrifice.

(4) Its ministry represents fulfillment (v. 24). The new covenant Christian has *reality!* We are not depending on a high priest on earth who annually visits the Holy of Holies in a temporary sanctuary. We depend on the heavenly High Priest who has entered once and for all into the eternal sanctuary. There He represents us before God, *and He always will.*

Beware of trusting anything for your spiritual life that is "made with hands" (Heb. 9:24). It will not last. The tabernacle was replaced by Solomon's temple, and that temple was destroyed by the Babylonians. When the Jews returned to their land after the captivity, they rebuilt their temple, and King Herod, in later years, expanded and embellished it. But the Romans destroyed that temple, and it has never been rebuilt. Furthermore, since the genealogical records have been lost or destroyed, the Jews are not certain who can minister as priests. These things that are "made with hands" are perishable, but the things "not made with hands" are eternal.

(5) Its ministry is final and complete (vv. 25–28). There can be nothing incomplete or temporary about our Lord's ministry in heaven. The writer points out again the obvious contrasts between the old covenant ministry and the new covenant ministry.

Old covenant	*New covenant*
Repeated sacrifices	One sacrifice
The blood of others	His own blood
Covering sin	Putting away sin
For Israel only	For all sinners
Left the Holy of Holies	Entered heaven and remains there
Came out to bless the people	Will come to take His people to heaven

In short, the work of Christ is a completed work, final and eternal. On the basis of His completed work, He is ministering now in heaven on our behalf.

Did you notice that the word *appear* is used three times in Hebrews 9:24–28? These three uses give us a summary of our Lord's work. He *has appeared* to put away sin by dying on the cross (Heb. 9:26). He *is appearing* now in heaven for us (Heb. 9:24). One day, He *shall appear* to take Christians home (Heb. 9:28). These "three tenses of salvation" are all based on His finished work.

After reading this chapter, the Hebrew Christians who received this letter had to realize that there is no middle ground. They had to make a choice between the earthly or the heavenly, the temporary or the eternal, the incomplete or the complete. *Why not return to the temple but also practice the*

Christian faith? Why not "the best of both worlds"? Because that would be compromising and refusing to go "without the camp, bearing his reproach" (Heb. 13:13). So there is no middle way.

The believer's sanctuary is in heaven. His Father is in heaven and his Savior is in heaven. His citizenship is in heaven (Phil. 3:20) and his treasures should be in heaven (Matt. 6:19ff.). And his hope is in heaven. The true believer walks by faith, not by sight. No matter what may happen on earth, a believer can be confident because everything is settled in heaven.

QUESTIONS FOR PERSONAL REFLECTION
OR GROUP DISCUSSION

1. What do you find to be challenging in keeping the balance between your earthly home and your heavenly home?

2. In the days of the Hebrew tabernacle God's very presence dwelled in the Holy of Holies. Today His presence is within us. In light of that, describe some practical ways in which the Israelites' experience with God was different from ours.

3. As a dwelling place for God, what were the limitations of the tabernacle?

4. What are the limitations of our lives and hearts as dwelling places for God?

5. The mercy seat reminded the Israelites of blood shed to cover their sins. What experiences or items in your life remind you of the mercy you were shown through Christ's blood?

6. Instead of covering our sin, Christ's blood removes our sin in God's sight. How do you think your life would be different today if your sin was covered rather than removed?

7. The Hebrew Christians were tempted to return to the Jewish ceremonial rites rather than stay with the new way that Christ was showing them. Identify some ways that we sometimes feel more comfortable with the familiar, even though it is not necessarily what God has ordained.

8. Review the items in the tabernacle. What lessons do you think God wanted to teach the Israelites through these items?

Chapter Nine

THE SUPERIOR SACRIFICE

(Hebrews 10)

A teenage boy, whose mother was away on a visit, found himself with time on his hands. He decided to read a book from the family library. His mother was a devout Christian, so the boy knew there would be a sermon at the beginning and an application at the end of the book, but there would also be some interesting stories in between.

While reading the book, he came across the phrase "the finished work of Christ." It struck him with unusual power. "The finished work of Christ."

"Why does the author use this expression?" he asked himself. "Why not say the atoning or the propitiatory work of Christ?" (You see, he knew all the biblical terms. He just did not know the Savior!) Then the words "It is finished" flashed into his mind, and he realized afresh that the work of salvation was accomplished.

"If the whole work was finished and the whole debt paid, what is there left for me to do?" He knew the answer and fell to his knees to receive the Savior and full forgiveness of sins. That is how J. Hudson Taylor, founder of the China Inland Mission (now OMF [Overseas Missionary Fellowship] International), was saved.

The tenth chapter of Hebrews emphasizes the perfect sacrifice of Jesus Christ, in contrast with the imperfect sacrifices that were offered under the old covenant. Our Lord's superior priesthood belongs to a better order—Melchizedek's and not Aaron's. It functions on the basis of a better covenant—the new covenant—and in a better sanctuary, in heaven. But all of this depends on the better sacrifice, which is the theme of this chapter.

The writer presents three benefits that explain why the sacrifice of Jesus Christ is superior to the old covenant sacrifices.

1. CHRIST'S SACRIFICE TAKES AWAY SIN (10:1–10)

Sin, of course, is man's greatest problem. No matter what kind of religion a man has, if it cannot deal with sin, it is of no value. By nature, man is a sinner, and by choice, he proves that his nature is sinful. It has well been said, "We are not sinners because we sin. We sin because we are sinners."

The need for a better sacrifice (vv. 1–4). Why were the old covenant sacrifices inferior? After all, they were ordained by the Lord, and they were in force for hundreds of years. While it is true that at times the Jewish people permitted these sacrifices to become empty rituals (Isa. 1:11–15), it is also true that many sincere people brought their offerings to God and were blessed.

The very *nature* of the old covenant sacrifices made them inferior. The law was only "a shadow of good things to come" and not the reality itself. The sacrificial system was a type or picture of the work our Lord would accomplish on the cross. This meant that the system was temporary, and therefore could accomplish nothing permanent. The very repetition of the sacrifices day after day, and the Day of Atonement year after year, pointed out the entire system's weaknesses.

Animal sacrifices could never completely deal with human guilt. God did promise forgiveness to believing worshippers (Lev. 4:20, 26, 31, 35), but this was a judicial forgiveness and not the removal of guilt from people's hearts. People lacked that inward witness of full and final forgiveness. They could not claim, "I have no more consciousness of sins." If those worshippers had been "once purged [from guilt of sin]" they would never again have had to offer another sacrifice.

So the annual Day of Atonement did not accomplish remission of sin but only "reminder of sin" (NIV). The annual repetition of the ceremony was evidence that the previous year's sacrifices had not done the job. True, the nation's sins were *covered*, but they were not *cleansed*. Nor did the people have God's inward witness of forgiveness and acceptance.

Yes, there was a desperate need for a better sacrifice because the blood of bulls and of goats could not take away sins. It could cover sin and postpone judgment, but it could never effect a once-and-for-all redemption. Only the better sacrifice of the Son of God could do that.

The provision of the better sacrifice (vv. 5–9). It was God who provided the sacrifice and not man. The quotation is from Psalm 40:6–8, and it is applied to Jesus Christ in His incarnation ("when he cometh into the world"). The quotation makes it clear that Jesus Christ is the fulfillment of the old covenant sacrifices.

The word *sacrifice* refers to any of the animal sacrifices. *Offering* covers the meal offering and the drink offering. The burnt offering and sin offering are mentioned (Heb. 10:6, 8). The trespass offering would be covered in the word *sacrifice* (Heb. 10:5). Each of these offerings typified the sacrifice of Christ and revealed some aspect of His work on the cross (see Lev. 1—7).

The phrase, "a body hast thou prepared me" (Heb. 10:5), is not found in the original quotation. Psalm 40:6 reads, "mine ears hast thou opened." The writer of Hebrews was quoting from the Septuagint, the

Greek translation of the Old Testament. How do we explain this variation? Some connect "mine ears hast thou opened" with Exodus 21:1–6, a passage that describes the actions of a master whose servant did not want to be set free. The master bored a hole through the earlobe of the servant, which was a sign that the servant preferred to remain with his master. The idea is that our Lord was like a willing servant who had His ears bored.

The problem with that explanation is that only *one* ear was bored, while the verse (Ps. 40:6) speaks of *both* ears. Furthermore, the verb used in Exodus 21 means "to pierce," while the verb in Psalm 40:6 means "to dig." Our Lord was a servant, but it is not likely that the writer had this in mind. Probably "opened ears" signified a readiness to hear and obey the will of God (see Isa. 50:4–6). God gave His Son a prepared body that the Son might serve God and fulfill His will on earth. Our Lord often referred to this truth (John 4:34; 5:30; 6:38; 17:4).

Of course, the same Holy Spirit who inspired Psalm 40 has the right to amplify and interpret His Word in Hebrews 10. "Opened ears" indicates a body ready for service.

Twice in this paragraph, the writer stated that God "had no pleasure" in the old covenant sacrifices (see Heb. 10:6, 8). This does not suggest that the old sacrifices were wrong, or that sincere worshippers received no benefit from obeying God's law. It only means that God had no delight in sacrifices as such, apart from the obedient hearts of the worshippers. No amount of sacrifices could substitute for obedience (1 Sam. 15:22, Ps. 51:16–17; Isa. 1:11, 19; Jer. 6:19–20; Hos. 6:6).

Jesus came to do the Father's will. This will is the new covenant that has replaced the old covenant. Through His death and resurrection, Jesus Christ has taken away the first covenant and established the second. The readers of this epistle called Hebrews would get the message: Why go back to a covenant that has been taken away? Why go back to sacrifices that are inferior?

The effectiveness of the better sacrifice (v. 10). Believers have been set apart ("sanctified") by the offering of Christ's body once for all. No old covenant sacrifice could do that. An old covenant worshipper had to be purified from ceremonial defilement repeatedly. But a new covenant saint is set apart finally and completely.

2. CHRIST'S SACRIFICE NEED NOT BE REPEATED (10:11–18)

Again the writer contrasted the old covenant high priest with Jesus Christ, our Great High Priest. The fact that Jesus *sat down* after He ascended to the Father is proof that His work was completed (Heb. 1:3, 13; 8:1). The ministry of the priests in the tabernacle and temple was *never done* and *never different:* They offered the same sacrifices day after day. This constant repetition was proof that their sacrifices did not take away sins. What tens of thousands of animal sacrifices could not accomplish, Jesus accomplished with *one sacrifice forever!*

The phrase "sat down" refers us again to Psalm 110:1: "Sit thou at my right hand, until I make thine enemies thy footstool." Christ is in the place of exaltation and victory. When He returns, He shall overcome every enemy and establish His righteous kingdom. Those who have trusted Him need not fear, for they have been "perfected for ever" (Heb. 10:14). Believers are "complete in him" (Col. 2:10). We have a perfect standing before God because of the finished work of Jesus Christ.

How do we know *personally* that we have this perfect standing before God? Because of the witness of the Holy Spirit through the Word (Heb. 10:15–18). The witness of the Spirit is based on the work of the Son and is given through the words of Scripture. The writer (Heb. 10:16–17) quotes Jeremiah 31:33–34, part of a passage he also quoted in Hebrews 8:7–12.

The old covenant worshipper could not say that he had "no more con-science of sins" (Heb. 10:2). But the new covenant believer *can* say that his sins and iniquities are remembered *no more.* There is "no more offering for sin" (Heb. 10:18) and no more remembrance of sin!

I once shared a conference with a fine Christian psychiatrist whose lectures were very true to the Word. "The trouble with psychiatry," he told me, "is that it can only deal with symptoms. A psychiatrist can remove a patient's *feelings* of guilt, but he cannot remove the guilt. It's like a trucker loosening a fender on his truck so he won't hear the motor knock. A patient can end up feeling better, but have *two* problems instead of one!"

When a sinner trusts Christ, his sins are all forgiven, the guilt is gone, and the matter is completely settled forever.

3. Christ's Sacrifice Opens the Way to God (10:19–39)

No old covenant worshipper would have been bold enough to try to enter the Holy of Holies in the tabernacle. Even the high priest entered the Holy of Holies only once a year. The thick veil that separated the Holy Place from the Holy of Holies was a barrier between people and God. Only the death of Christ could tear that veil (Mark 15:38) and open the way into the *heavenly* sanctuary where God dwells.

A gracious invitation (vv. 19–25). "Let us draw near…. Let us hold fast…. Let us consider one another." This threefold invitation hinges on our boldness to enter into the holiest. And this boldness ("freedom of speech") rests on the finished work of the Savior. On the Day of Atonement, the high priest could not enter the Holy of Holies unless he had the blood of the sacrifice (Heb. 9:7). But our entrance into God's presence is not because of an animal's blood, but because of Christ's shed blood.

This open way into God's presence is "new" (recent, fresh) and not a part of the old covenant that "waxeth [grows] old [and] is ready to vanish away" (Heb. 8:13). It is "living" because Christ "ever liveth to make inter-cession" for us (Heb. 7:25). Christ is the "new and living way"! We come to God through Him, our High Priest over the house of God (the church, see Heb. 3:6). When His flesh was torn on the cross, and His life sacrificed, God tore the veil in the temple. This symbolized the new and living way now opened for all who believe.

On the basis of these assurances—that we have boldness to enter because we have a living High Priest—we have an "open invitation" to enter the presence of God. The old covenant high priest *visited* the Holy of Holies once a year, but we are invited to *dwell in the presence of God* every moment of each day. What a tremendous privilege! Consider what is involved in this threefold invitation.

(1) Let us draw near (v. 22). Of course, we must prepare ourselves spir-itually to fellowship with God. The Old Testament priest had to go through various washings and the applying of blood on the Day of Atone-ment (Lev. 16). Also, during the regular daily ministry, the priests had to wash at the laver before they entered the Holy Place (Ex. 30:18–21). The New Testament Christian must come to God with a pure heart and a clean conscience. Fellowship with God demands purity (1 John 1:5—2:2).

(2) Let us hold fast (v. 23). The readers of this epistle were being tempted to forsake their confession of Jesus Christ by going back to the old covenant worship. The writer did not exhort them to hold on to their salvation, because their security was in Christ and not in themselves (Heb. 7:25). Rather, he invited them to hold fast "the profession [con-fession] of ... hope." (There is no manuscript evidence for the word *faith*. The Greek word is *hope*.)

We have noted in our study of Hebrews that there is an emphasis on the glorious hope of the believer. God is "bringing many sons unto glory" (Heb. 2:10). Believers are "partakers of the heavenly calling" (Heb. 3:1) and therefore can rejoice in hope (Heb. 3:6). *Hope* is one of the main themes of Hebrews 6 (vv. 11–12, 18–20). We are looking for Christ to return (Heb. 9:28), and we are seeking that city that is yet to come (Heb. 13:14).

When a believer has his hope fixed on Christ and relies on the faithfulness of God, then he will not waver. Instead of looking back (as the Jews so often did), we should look ahead to the coming of the Lord.

(3) Let us consider one another (vv. 24–25). Fellowship with God must never become selfish. We must also fellowship with other Christians in the local assembly. Apparently, some of the wavering believers had been absenting themselves from the church fellowship. It is interesting to note that the emphasis here is not on what a believer *gets from* the assembly, but rather on what he can *contribute to* the assembly. Faithfulness in church attendance encourages others and provokes them to love and good works. One of the strong motives for faithfulness is the soon coming of Jesus Christ. In fact, the only other place the word translated "assembling" (Heb. 10:25) is used in the New Testament is in 2 Thessalonians 2:1, where it's translated "gathering" and deals with the coming of Christ.

The three great Christian virtues are evidenced here: *faith* (Heb. 10:22), *hope* (Heb. 10:23), and *love* (Heb. 10:24). They are the fruit of our fellowship with God in His heavenly sanctuary.

A solemn exhortation (vv. 26–31). This is the fourth of the five exhortations found in Hebrews. It is written to believers and follows in sequence with the other exhortations. The believer who begins to *drift* from the Word (Heb. 2:1–4) will soon start to *doubt* the Word (Heb. 3:7—4:13). Soon, he will become *dull* toward the Word (Heb. 5:11—6:20) and become "lazy" in his spiritual life. This will result in *despising* the Word, which is the theme of this exhortation.

The evidence of this "despising" is willful sin. The tense of the verb indicates that Hebrews 10:26 should read, "For if we willfully *go on sinning.*" This exhortation is not dealing with one particular act of sin, but with an attitude that leads to repeated disobedience. Under the old covenant, there were no sacrifices for deliberate and willful sins (Ex. 21:12–14; Num. 15:27–31). Presumptuous sinners who despised Moses' law and broke it were executed (Deut. 17:1–7). This explains why David prayed as he did in Psalm 51. Because he deliberately sinned with a high hand, he should have been slain, but he cried out for God's mercy. David knew that even a multitude of sacrifices could not save him. All he could offer was the sacrifice of a broken heart (Ps. 51:16–17).

How does an arrogant attitude affect a believer's relationship with God? It is as though he treads Jesus Christ underfoot, cheapens the precious blood that saved him ("an unholy thing" [Heb. 10:29] = "a common thing"), and insults the Holy Spirit. This is just the opposite of the exhortation given in Hebrews 10:19–25! Instead of having a bold profession of faith, hope, and love, a backslidden believer so lives that his actions and attitudes bring disgrace to the name of Christ and the church.

What can this kind of a Christian expect from God? He can expect severe discipline. (Chastening is the theme of Heb. 12.) There is no need to water down words such as "judgment and fiery indignation" (Heb. 10:27), or "sorer punishment" (Heb. 10:29). We have already seen from the history of Israel that hardly anybody who was saved out of Egypt by the blood of the lamb entered into the promised inheritance. Nearly all of them died in the wilderness. "There is a sin unto death" (1 John 5:16). Some of the Corinthian believers were disciplined and their lives taken because of their presumptuous sins (1 Cor. 11:30, where "sleep" means "died").

God does not always take the life of a rebellious believer, but He always deals with him. "To me belongeth vengeance" was spoken to Israel, God's people (Deut. 32:35). "The Lord shall judge his people" (Heb. 10:30)! "It is a fearful thing to fall into the hands of the living God" (Heb. 10:31).

The major theme of Hebrews is "God has spoken—how are you responding to His Word?" When the nation of Israel refused to believe and obey His Word, God chastened them. Paul used this fact to warn the Corinthians against presumptuous sins (1 Cor. 10:1–12). Note that the examples given in this passage involve people who died because of their willful sins. When we study the subject of "chastening" in Hebrews 12, we will get greater insight into this awesome aspect of God's dealings with His children.

In stating that this exhortation applies to believers today, but that it does not involve loss of salvation, I am not suggesting that chastening is unimportant. On the contrary, it is important that every Christian obey God and please the Father in all things. Dr. William Culbertson, late president of the Moody Bible Institute, used to warn us about "the sad consequences of *forgiven sins.*" God forgave David's sins, but David suffered the sad consequences for years afterward (2 Sam. 12:7–15). David had "despised the commandment of the Lord" (2 Sam. 12:9), and God dealt with him.

What should a believer do who has drifted away into spiritual doubt and dullness and is deliberately despising God's Word? He should turn to God for mercy and forgiveness. There is no other sacrifice for sin, but the sacrifice Christ made is sufficient for all our sins. It is a fearful thing to fall into the Lord's hands for chastening, but it is a wonderful thing to fall into His hands for cleansing and restoration. David said, "Let me fall now into the hand of the Lord; for very great are his mercies" (1 Chron. 21:13).

An encouraging confirmation (vv. 32–39). Lest any of his readers should misinterpret his exhortation, the writer followed it with words of encouragement and confirmation. His readers had given every evidence that they were true Christians. He did not expect them to despise God's Word and experience the chastening of God! In fact, as in Hebrews 6, the writer shifted the pronouns from "we" in Hebrews 10:26 to "he" in Hebrews 10:29 and "them" in Hebrews 10:39.

The readers had been willing to suffer reproach and persecution, even to the spoiling of their goods. When they were not being persecuted themselves, they courageously identified with the other Christians who were in danger, even to the point of sharing their bonds (imprisonment). At that time, they had great confidence and hope, but now they were in danger of casting away that confidence and going back into their old religion.

The secret of victory was in their *faith* and *patience* ("courageous endurance"). We have met this combination of graces in Hebrews 6:12, 15. It is here that the writer introduced the "text" around which Hebrews is written: "The just shall live by faith" (Heb. 10:38). The quotation is from Habakkuk 2:4, and it is also used in Romans 1:17 and Galatians 3:11. Romans emphasizes "the just," Galatians deals with "shall live," and Hebrews centers on "by faith." We are not just *saved* from our sin by faith; we also must *live* by faith. This is the theme of Hebrews 11—13.

The believer who lives by faith will "go on unto perfection" (Heb. 6:1). But the believer who lives by sight will "draw back unto perdition" (Heb. 10:39). What is "perdition" in this context? The Greek word translated "perdition" is used about twenty times in the New Testament and is translated by different words: "perish" (Acts 8:20), "die" (Acts 25:16), "destruction" (Rom. 9:22), and "waste" (Matt. 26:8). The word *can* mean eternal judgment, but it need not in *every* instance. I personally believe that "waste" is the best translation for this word in Hebrews 10:39. A believer who does not walk by faith goes back into the old ways and wastes his life.

"The saving of the soul" is the opposite of "waste." To walk by faith means to obey God's Word and live for Jesus Christ. We lose our lives for His sake—but we save them (see Matt. 16:25–27)! In my own pastoral ministry, I have met people who turned their backs on God's will and (like Israel) spent years "wandering in the wilderness" of waste.

But we can be confident! As we walk by faith, our Great High Priest will guide us and perfect us!

QUESTIONS FOR PERSONAL REFLECTION
OR GROUP DISCUSSION

1. What keeps us from accepting that Christ's work of salvation is a "finished work"?

2. Wiersbe quotes, "We are not sinners because we sin. We sin because we are sinners." What does he mean? Why do you agree or disagree with that statement?

3. The sin sacrifices served not to remove sin, but to remind the people of their sin. What do you do to remind yourself that you have sin that needs to be dealt with?

4. Why was blood such a significant part of sacrifices?

5. List some things you look forward to about Christ's return.

6. Think of a time when you believe you were "chastened" by the Lord. How did you realize what was happening?

7. How would you define "deliberate and willful sin" in today's language and with modern examples?

8. Habakkuk 2:4 says, "The just shall live by his faith." What does "living by faith" mean for you?

9. What are some examples of *not* living by faith?

10. Give some examples of circumstances you may face this week that will require faith on your part.

Chapter Ten

FAITH—THE GREATEST POWER IN THE WORLD

(Hebrews 11)

T his chapter introduces the final section of the epistle (Heb. 11—13), which I have called "A Superior Principle—Faith." The fact that Christ is a superior person (Heb. 1—6) and that He exercises a superior priesthood (Heb. 7—10) ought to encourage us to put our trust in Him. The readers of this epistle were being tempted to go back into Judaism and put their faith in Moses. Their confidence was in the visible things of this world, not the invisible realities of God. Instead of going on to perfection (maturity), they were going "back unto perdition [waste]" (Heb. 6:1; 10:39).

In Hebrews 11, all Christians are called to live by faith. In it, the writer discusses two important topics relating to faith.

1. THE DESCRIPTION OF FAITH (11:1–3)

This is not a definition of faith but a description of what faith does and how it works. True Bible faith is not blind optimism or a manufactured "hope-so" feeling. Neither is it an intellectual assent to a doctrine. It is certainly not believing in spite of evidence! That would be superstition.

True Bible faith is confident obedience to God's Word in spite of circumstances and consequences. Read that last sentence again and let it soak into your mind and heart.

This faith operates quite simply. God speaks and we hear His Word. We trust His Word and act on it no matter what the circumstances are or what the consequences may be. The circumstances may be impossible, and the consequences frightening and unknown; but we obey God's Word just the same and believe Him to do what is right and what is best.

The unsaved world does not understand true Bible faith, probably because it sees so little faith in action in the church today. The cynical editor H. L. Mencken defined faith as "illogical belief in the occurrence of the improbable." The world fails to realize that faith is only as good as its object, and the object of our faith is *God.* Faith is not some "feeling" that we manufacture. It is our total response to what God has revealed in His Word.

Three words in Hebrews 11:1–3 summarize what true Bible faith is: *substance, evidence,* and *witness.* The word translated "substance" means literally "to stand under, to support." Faith is to a Christian what a foundation is to a house: It gives confidence and assurance that he will stand. So you might say, "Faith is the confidence of things hoped for." When a believer has faith, it is God's way of giving him confidence and assurance that what is promised will be experienced.

The word *evidence* simply means "conviction." This is the inward conviction from God that what He has promised, He will perform. The presence of God-given faith in one's heart is conviction enough that He will keep His Word.

Witness ("obtained a good report") is an important word in Hebrews 11. It occurs not only in verse 2, but also once in verse 4 and once in verse 39. The summary in Hebrews 12:1 calls this list of men and women "so great a cloud of witnesses." They are witnesses to us because God witnessed to them. In each example cited, God gave witness to that person's faith. This witness was His divine approval on their lives and ministries.

The writer of Hebrews made it clear that faith is a very practical thing (Heb. 11:3), in spite of what unbelievers say. Faith enables us to understand what God does. Faith enables us to see what others cannot see (note Heb. 11:7, 13, 27). As a result, faith enables us to do what others cannot do! People laughed at these great men and women when they stepped out by faith, but God was with them and enabled them to succeed to His glory. Dr. J. Oswald Sanders put it perfectly: "Faith enables the believing soul to treat the future as present and the invisible as seen."

The best way to grow in faith is to walk with the faithful. The remainder of this chapter is devoted to a summary of the lives and labors of great men and women of faith found in the Old Testament. In each instance, you will find the same elements of faith: (1) God spoke to them through His Word; (2) their inner selves were stirred in different ways; (3) they obeyed God; (4) He bore witness about them.

2. THE DEMONSTRATION OF FAITH (11:4–40)

Abel—faith worshipping (v. 4). The background story is in Genesis 4:1–10. Abel was a righteous man because of faith (Matt. 23:35). God had revealed to Adam and his descendants the true way of worship, and Abel obeyed God by faith. In fact, his obedience cost him his life. Cain was not a child of God (1 John 3:10–12) because he did not have faith. He was religious but not righteous. Abel speaks to us today as the first martyr of the faith.

Enoch—faith walking (vv. 5–6). Our faith in God grows as we fellowship with God. We must have both the *desire* to please Him and the *diligence* to seek Him. Prayer, meditating on the Word, worship, discipline—all of these help us in our walk with God. Enoch walked with God in the wicked world, before the flood came; he was able to keep his life pure. Enoch was taken to heaven one day ("translated" = "carried across") and seen no more. Abel died a violent death, but Enoch never died. God has a different plan for each one who trusts Him. Some see in the translation of Enoch a picture of the rapture of the church when Jesus Christ returns (1 Thess. 4:13–18).

Noah—faith working (v. 7). Noah's faith involved the whole person: His *mind* was warned of God; his *heart* was moved with fear; and his *will* acted on what God told him. Since nobody at that time had ever seen a flood (or perhaps even a rainstorm), Noah's actions must have generated a great deal of interest and probably ridicule as well. Noah's faith influenced his whole family and they were saved. It also condemned the whole world, for his faith revealed their unbelief. Events proved that Noah was right! Jesus used this experience to warn people to be ready for His return (Matt. 24:36–42). In Noah's day, the people were involved in innocent everyday activities and completely ignored Noah's witness (2 Peter 2:5).

The patriarchs—faith waiting (vv. 8–22). The emphasis in this section is on the promise of God and His plans for the nation of Israel (Heb. 11:9, 11, 13, 17). The nation began with the call of Abraham. God promised Abraham and Sarah a son, but they had to wait twenty-five years for the fulfillment of the promise. Their son Isaac became the father of Jacob and Esau, and it was Jacob who really built the nation through the birth of his twelve sons. Joseph saved the nation *in* the land of Egypt, and Moses would later deliver them *from* Egypt.

Waiting is, for me, one of the most difficult disciplines of life. Yet true faith is able to wait for the fulfillment of God's purposes *in God's time.* But, while we are waiting, we must also be obeying. "By faith Abraham … obeyed" (Heb. 11:8). He obeyed when *he did not know where he was going* (Heb. 11:8–10). He lived in tents because he was a stranger and pilgrim in the world and had to be ready to move whenever God spoke. Christians today are also strangers and pilgrims (1 Peter 1:1; 2:11). Abraham had his eyes on the heavenly city and lived in the future tense.

He also obeyed when *he did not know how God's will would be accomplished* (Heb. 11:11–12). Both Abraham and Sarah were too old to have children. Yet they both believed that God would do the miracle (Rom. 4:13–25). Unbelief asks, "How *can* this be?" (see Luke 1:18–20). Faith asks, "How *shall* this be?" (Luke 1:34–37).

Abraham believed and obeyed God when *he did not know when God would fulfill His promises* (Heb. 11:13–16). None of the patriarchs saw the complete fulfillment of God's promises, but they saw from "afar off" what God was doing. Dr. George Morrison, a great Scottish preacher, once said, "The important thing is not what we live in, but what we look for." These men and women of faith lived in tents, but they knew a heavenly city awaited them. God always fulfills His promises to His believing people, either immediately or ultimately.

Finally, Abraham obeyed God by faith when *he did not know why God was so working* (Heb. 11:17–19). Why would God want Abraham to sacrifice his son when it was the Lord who gave him that son? All of a future nation's promises were wrapped up in Isaac. The tests of faith become more difficult as we walk with God, yet the rewards are more wonderful! And we must not ignore the obedient faith of Isaac.

In Abraham, Isaac, Jacob, and Joseph, we have four generations of faith. These men sometimes failed, but basically they were men of faith. They were not perfect, but they were devoted to God and trusted His Word. Isaac passed the promises and the blessings along to Jacob (Gen. 27), and Jacob shared them with his twelve sons (Gen. 48—49). Jacob was a pilgrim, for even as he was dying he leaned on his pilgrim staff.

The faith of Joseph was certainly remarkable. After the way his family treated him, you would think he would have abandoned his faith, but instead, it grew stronger. Even the ungodly influence of Egypt did not weaken his trust in God. Joseph did not use his family, his job, or his circumstances as an excuse for unbelief. *Joseph knew what he believed*—that God would one day deliver his people from Egypt (Gen. 50:24–26). *Joseph also knew where he belonged*—in Canaan, not in Egypt, so he made them promise to carry his remains out of Egypt at the exodus. They did (see Ex. 13:19 and Josh. 24:32)!

We have to admire the faith of the patriarchs. They did not have a complete Bible, and yet their faith was strong. They handed God's promises down from one generation to another. In spite of their failures and testings, these men and women believed God, and He bore witness to their faith. How much more faith you and I should have!

Moses—faith warring (vv. 23–29). Moses was fortunate to have believing parents. For them to hide their baby son from the authorities was certainly an act of faith. The account is given in Exodus 2:1–10. Moses' parents were named Amram and Jochebed (Ex. 6:20). Though godly parents cannot pass on their faith as they do family traits, they can certainly create an atmosphere of faith at home and be examples to their children. A home should be the first school of faith for a child.

Three great themes relating to faith are seen in the life of Moses. First, *the refusal of faith* (Heb. 11:24–25). As the adopted son of the Egyptian princess, Moses could have led an easy life in the palace. But his faith moved him to refuse that kind of life. He chose to identify with God's suffering people. True faith causes a believer to hold the right values and make the right decisions. The phrase "pleasures of sin" does not refer only to lust and other gross sins. The phrase describes a way of life that we today would call "successful"—position, prestige, power, wealth, and freedom from problems.

Moses' refusal of faith led to *the reproach of faith* (Heb. 11:26a). The mayor of a large American city moved into a dangerous and decayed housing project to demonstrate the problems and needs of the minorities. But she also kept her fashionable apartment and eventually moved out of the slum. We commend her for her courage, but we have to admire Moses even more. He left the palace *and never went back to the old life!* He identified with the Jewish slaves! Men and women of faith often have to bear reproach and suffering. The apostles suffered for their faith. Contemporary believers behind the Iron Curtain knew what it was to bear reproach. If reproach is an evidence of true faith, we wonder how much true faith there is in our own country today!

Finally, there is *the reward of faith* (Heb. 11:26b–29). God always rewards true faith—if not immediately, at least ultimately. Over against "the treasures in Egypt" Moses saw the "recompense of the reward." As Dr. Vance Havner said, "Moses chose the imperishable, saw the invisible, and did the impossible." Moses' faith enabled him to face Pharaoh unafraid, and to trust God to deal with the enemy. The endurance of Moses was not a natural gift, for by nature Moses was hesitant and retiring. This endurance and courage came as the reward of his faith.

The faith of Moses was rewarded with deliverance for him and his people. (See Ex. 11—13 for the exciting Passover account.) Faith brings us *out* (Heb. 11:28), takes us *through* (Heb. 11:29), and brings us *in* (Heb. 11:30). When we trust God, we get what God can do, but when we trust ourselves, we get only what weak people can do. The experience of Moses is proof that true biblical faith means obeying God in spite of circumstances and in spite of consequences.

If you and I had been writing this chapter, the next section would be *faith wandering*—but there is no mention of Israel's failure and forty years of wasted time. Why? Because that was an experience of *unbelief,* not faith! The writer did use this experience in Hebrews 3 and 4 as an illustration of doubting the Word. But nowhere in Hebrews 11 will you find a record of *any* failure because of unbelief. Faith records only the victories.

Joshua and Rahab—faith winning (vv. 30–31). The account of the conquest of Jericho is found in Joshua 2—6. Joshua was Moses' successor as leader of Israel, and he succeeded because he trusted the same God that Moses had trusted. God changes His workmen, but He does not change His principles of operation. He blesses faith and He judges unbelief.

From a human point of view, Jericho was an impossible city to conquer. However, Joshua's first act of faith was not the defeat of the city, but the crossing of the Jordan River. By faith, the nation crossed the river just as the previous generation had crossed the Red Sea. This was a witness and a warning to the Canaanite nations that Israel was marching forward by the power of God.

Rahab was a harlot, an unlikely person to put faith in the true God of Israel. *She was saved by grace,* because the other inhabitants of the city were marked out for death. God in His mercy and grace permitted Rahab to live. But *she was saved by faith.* What she knew about God is recorded in Joshua 2:8–14. She knew that Jehovah had delivered Israel from Egypt and that He had opened the Red Sea. But that was forty years before! She also knew God had defeated the other nations during Israel's wilderness wanderings. "For the LORD your God, he is God in heaven above, and in earth beneath" (Josh. 2:11). That was her testimony of faith, and God honored it.

She was saved unto good works. True faith must always show itself in good works (James 2:20–26). She protected the spies, put the cord in the window as directed (Josh. 2:15–21), apparently won her family to the true faith (Josh. 2:13; 6:25), and in every way obeyed the Lord. Not only was Rahab delivered from judgment, but she became a part of the nation of Israel. She married Salmon and gave birth to Boaz who was an ancestor of King David (Matt. 1:4–6). Imagine a pagan harlot becoming a part of the ancestry of Jesus Christ! That is what faith can do!

Rahab is certainly a rebuke to unsaved people who give excuses for not trusting Christ. "I don't know very much about the Bible" is an excuse I often hear. Rahab knew very little spiritual truth, but she acted on what she did know. "I am too bad to be saved!" is another excuse. But Rahab was a condemned heathen harlot! Another excuse is "What will my family think?" Rahab's first concern was *saving* her family, not opposing them. She stands as one of the great women of faith in the Bible.

Various heroes of faith (vv. 32–40). Faith can operate in the life of any person who will dare to listen to God's Word and surrender to God's will. What a variety of personalities we have here! Gideon was a frightened farmer whose faith did not grow strong right away (Judg. 6:11—7:25). Barak won a resounding victory over Sisera, but he needed Deborah the prophetess as his helper to assure him (see Judg. 4:1—5:31). Both Gideon and Barak are encouragements to us who falter in our faith.

The story of Samson is familiar (Judg. 13—16). We would not call Samson a godly man, for he yielded to his fleshly appetites. He was a Nazarite, which meant he was dedicated to God and was never to cut his hair or partake of the fruit of the vine. (A Nazarite should not be confused with a Nazarene, a resident of Nazareth.) Samson did trust God to help and deliver him and, in the end, Samson was willing to give his life to defeat the enemy. However, we must not conclude that believers today can expect to lead double lives and still enjoy God's blessing.

Jephthah's story is fascinating (Judg. 11:1—12:7). It is unlikely that he sacrificed his only daughter as a burnt offering, for this was forbidden in Israel. Probably he dedicated her to the Lord on the basis of the "law of vows" (Lev. 27), dedicating her to perpetual virginity (Judg. 11:34–40).

It is not possible for us to examine each example of faith, and even the writer of Hebrews stopped citing names after he mentioned David and Samuel, who were certainly great men of faith. There are examples in the

Old Testament of men and women who won the victories referred to in Hebrews 11:33–35. David certainly subdued kingdoms and wrought righteousness. Daniel's faith "stopped the mouths of lions" (see Dan. 6), and the three Hebrew children overcame the power of the fiery furnace (Dan. 3:23–28). The women of faith mentioned in Hebrews 11:35 have their stories given in 1 Kings 17:17–24 and 2 Kings 4:18–37.

The transition in Hebrews 11:35 is important: Not all men and women of faith experienced miraculous deliverance. Some were tortured and died! The word translated "others" in Hebrews 11:36 means "others of a different land." These "others" had faith, but God did not see fit to deal with them in the same way he dealt with Moses, Gideon, and David.

While making a hospital visit, I found a patient lying in bed weeping. "What's the matter?" I asked. Her reply was to hand me a book that she had that day received in the mail. It was on "divine healing" and "the power of faith." Some anonymous person had written on the flyleaf, "Read this book—it will give you faith to be healed." The patient happened to be a dedicated Christian who trusted God even in the midst of suffering. But her anonymous correspondent thought that *all* people with faith should be delivered miraculously.

I have personally experienced God's miracle touch on my body when others were sure I would die. I know that God can heal. But I also know that God *does not have to heal* in order to prove that I have faith. The writer of Hebrews (11:36–38) recorded the fact that many unknown men and women of faith *were not delivered* from difficult circumstances, yet God honored their faith. In fact, it takes more faith to *endure* than it does to *escape*. Like the three Hebrew children, we should trust God and obey Him *even if He does not deliver us* (Dan. 3:16–18).

Man's estimate of these heroes of faith was a low one, so men persecuted them, arrested them, tortured them, and in some cases, killed them.

But God's estimate is entirely different. He said that the world was not worthy of these people! The apostle Paul is a good illustration of this truth. Festus said that Paul was out of his mind (Acts 26:24). The Jews said Paul was not fit to live (Acts 22:22). Paul himself said he was treated like "the filth of the world ... the offscouring of all things" (1 Cor. 4:13). Yet Paul was God's chosen vessel, probably the greatest Christian who ever lived!

Faith enables us to turn from the approval of the world and seek only the approval of God. If God is glorified by delivering His people, He will do it. If He sees fit to be glorified by *not* delivering His people, then He will do that. But we must never conclude that the absence of deliverance means a lack of faith on the part of God's children.

Faith looks to the future, for that is where the greatest rewards are found. The people named in this chapter (and those unnamed) did not receive "the promises" ("what was promised" [Heb. 11:13]) but they had God's witness to their faith that one day they would be rewarded. God's purpose involves Old Testament saints as well as New Testament saints! One day all of us shall share that heavenly city that true saints look for by faith.

We today should give thanks for these saints of old, for they were faithful during difficult times, and yet *we* are the ones who have received the "better blessing." They saw some of these blessings afar off (see John 8:56 NIV), but we enjoy them today through Jesus Christ. If the saints of old had not trusted God and obeyed His will, Israel would have perished and the Messiah would not have been born.

"Without faith it is impossible to please [God]" (Heb. 11:6). But this kind of faith grows as we listen to His Word (Rom. 10:17) and fellowship in worship and prayer. Faith is possible to all kinds of believers in all kinds of situations. It is not a luxury for a few elite saints. It is a necessity for all of God's people.

Lord, increase our faith!

QUESTIONS FOR PERSONAL REFLECTION
OR GROUP DISCUSSION

1. What are the invisible things you have faith in?

2. Wiersbe says Cain was "religious but not righteous." Define the difference between the two. Do you tend more to be religious or to be righteous?

3. Think of a time when you were left waiting, not knowing what the outcome of a situation would be. How did that affect your faith?

4. Compare Rahab's comments about God (Josh. 2:8–14) with the Israelites' comments (Deut. 1:27–28). How would you describe the difference between Rahab's faith and the Israelites' faith?

5. Think about the faith of the "others" in verse 36 who did not receive miracles or liberation for their faith. Instead they suffered and even died. Why does it make sense to hold to your faith even if it doesn't bring you deliverance from your suffering?

6. How do you make sense in your mind, and according to Scripture, of a situation where a person prays to be healed and has full faith that God can heal, but healing doesn't come?

7. Why have so many people in our world been persecuted for their faith?

8. Describe a time when you have seen someone's faith change his or her circumstances.

9. "Without faith it is impossible to please [God]" (Heb. 11:6). What is your response to that truth?

Chapter Eleven

STAY IN THE RUNNING!

(Hebrews 12)

If the apostle Paul were alive today, he would probably read the sports pages of the newspaper and follow the progress of various teams and athletes. Why? Because several athletic references in his letters indicate his interest in sports. Of course, both the Greeks and the Romans were keenly interested in athletic contests, not only for their physical well-being, but also for the honor of their towns and countries. It was a patriotic thing to be a good athlete and to bring glory to your country.

The writer of Hebrews combined these two themes of athletics and citizenship in this important twelfth chapter. The atmosphere is that of the footraces in the arena. We can see the runners laying aside their training weights and striving to run their races successfully. Some get weary and faint, while others endure to the end and win the prize. First the writer pictures the race (Heb. 12:1–13), and then emphasizes citizenship in the heavenly city (Heb. 12:14–29). In the minds of his readers, these two themes would go together, for no one could take part in the official games unless he was a citizen of the nation.

The one theme that runs through this chapter is *endurance* (Heb. 12:1 ["patience"], 2–3, 7; also see 10:32, 36 ["patience"]). The Jewish believers who received this letter were getting weary and wanted to give up; but the writer encouraged them to keep moving forward in their Christian lives, like runners on a track (see Phil. 3:12–14). He pointed out three divine resources that encourage a Christian to keep going when the situation is difficult.

1. THE EXAMPLE OF THE SON OF GOD (12:1–4)

When I was in junior high school, I had a coach who felt it his duty to make an athlete out of me. Everybody in my class could have told him he was wasting his time, because I was the worst athlete in the class—perhaps in the school! I entered a city-wide school competition, running the low hurdles. I knocked down six hurdles, fractured my left ankle, and immediately abandoned my sports career. (Shortly after, the coach enlisted in the army. I may have driven him to it.)

Coach Walker used several techniques to get me to do my best. "Other students have done it, and so can you!" was one of his encouragements. "Just think of what it will do for you physically!" was another. "Now, watch the other kids—see how they do it!" was a third. As I reflect on this experience, I am amazed to discover that these same three approaches are used in this paragraph to encourage us in the Christian race.

(1) **Look around at the winners (v. 1a)!** The "great … cloud [assembly, mass] of witnesses" was introduced to us in Hebrews 11. They are the heroes of the faith. It is not suggested here that these men and women now in heaven are watching us as we run the race, like people seated in a stadium. The word "witnesses" does not mean "spectators." Our English word *martyr* comes directly from the Greek word translated "witness." These people are not witnessing what we are doing; rather, they are bearing witness *to us* that God can see us through. God bore witness to them (Heb. 11:2, 4–5, 39) and they are bearing witness now to us.

"I rarely read the Old Testament, except for Psalms and Proverbs," a believer once told me.

"Then you are missing a great deal of spiritual help," I replied. I asked him to open to Romans 15:4 and read the verse aloud.

"For whatsoever things were written aforetime were written for our learning, that we through patience and comfort of the scriptures might have hope."

I then explained that *patience* means "endurance," and that *comfort* means "encouragement." One of the best ways to develop endurance and encouragement is to get to know the godly men and women of the Old Testament who ran the race and won. If you are having problems with your family, read about Joseph. If you think your job is too big for you, study the life of Moses. If you are tempted to retaliate, see how David handled this problem.

(2) Look at yourself (v. 1b)! Athletes used to wear training weights to help them prepare for the events. No athlete would actually participate wearing the weights because they would slow him down. (The modern analogy is a baseball player who swings a bat with a heavy metal collar on it before he steps to the plate.) Too much weight would tax one's endurance.

What are the "weights" that we should remove so that we might win the race? Everything that hinders our progress. They might even be "good things" in the eyes of others. A winning athlete does not choose between the good and the bad; he chooses between the better and the best.

We should also get rid of "the sin that so easily entangles" (Heb. 12:1 NIV). While he does not name any specific sin, the writer was probably referring to the sin of unbelief. It was unbelief that kept Israel out of the Promised Land, and it is unbelief that hinders us from entering into our spiritual inheritance in Christ. The phrase "by faith" (or "through faith") is used twenty-one times in Hebrews 11, indicating that it is faith in Christ that enables us to endure.

(3) Look at Jesus Christ (vv. 2–4)! He is "the author [originator] and finisher of our faith." It was in "looking unto Jesus" that we were saved, for *to look* means "to trust." When the dying Jews looked to the uplifted serpent, they were healed, and this is an illustration of our salvation through faith in Christ (Num. 21:4–9; John 3:14–16). "Looking unto Jesus" describes an *attitude* of faith and not just a single act.

When our Lord was here on earth, He lived by faith. The mystery of His divine and human natures is too profound for us to understand fully, but we do know that He had to trust His Father in heaven as He lived day by day. The writer of Hebrews quoted our Lord saying, "I will put my trust in him" (Heb. 2:13). (The quotation is from Isa. 8:17.) The fact that Jesus *prayed* is evidence that He lived by faith.

Our Lord endured far more than did any of the heroes of faith named in Hebrews 11, and therefore He is a perfect example for us to follow. *He endured the cross!* This involved shame, suffering, the "contradiction [opposition] of sinners," and even temporary rejection by the Father. On the cross He suffered for *all* the sins of *all* the world! Yet He endured and finished the work the Father gave Him to do (John 17:4). Though the readers of Hebrews had suffered persecution, they had not yet "resisted unto blood" (Heb. 12:4). None of them was yet a martyr. But in Jesus' battle against sin, He shed His own blood.

What was it that enabled our Lord to endure the cross? Please keep in mind that during His ministry on earth, our Lord did not use His divine powers for His own personal needs. Satan tempted Him to do this (Matt. 4:1–4), but Jesus refused. It was our Lord's *faith* that enabled Him to endure. He kept the eye of faith on "the joy that was set before him." From Psalm 16:8–10, He knew that He would come out of the tomb alive. (Peter referred to this messianic psalm in his sermon at Pentecost, Acts 2:24–33.) In that psalm (16:11) David spoke about "fullness of joy" in the presence of the Father. Also, from Psalm 110:1, 4, Jesus knew that He would be exalted to heaven in glory. (Peter also quoted this psalm, Acts 2:34–36.) So "the joy that was set before him" would include Jesus' completing the Father's will, His resurrection and exaltation, and His joy in presenting believers to the Father in glory (Jude 24).

Throughout this epistle, the writer emphasized the importance of the *future hope.* His readers were prone to *look back* and want to *go back,* but he encouraged them to follow Christ's example and *look ahead* by faith. The heroes of faith named in the previous chapter lived for the future, and this enabled them to endure (Heb. 11:10, 14–16, 24–27). Like Peter, when we get our eyes of faith off the Savior, we start to sink (Matt. 14:22–33).

Since Christ is the "author and finisher of our faith," trusting Him releases His power in our lives. I could try to follow the example of some great athlete for years and still be a failure. But if, in my younger days, that athlete could have entered into my life and shared his know-how and ability with me, that would have made me a winner. Christ is both the exemplar *and the enabler!* As we see Him in the Word and yield to His Spirit, He increases our faith and enables us to run the race.

2. THE ASSURANCE OF THE LOVE OF GOD (12:5–13)

The key word in this section is *chastening.* It is a Greek word that means "child training, instruction, discipline." A Greek boy was expected to "work out" in the gymnasium until he reached his maturity. It was a part of his preparation for adult life. The writer viewed the trials of the Christian life as spiritual discipline that could help a believer mature. Instead of trying to escape the difficulties of life, we should rather be "exercised" by them so that we might grow (Heb. 12:11).

When we are suffering, it is easy to think that God does not love us. So the writer gave three proofs that chastening comes from the Father's heart of love.

(1) The Scriptures (vv. 5–6). The quotation is from Proverbs 3:11–12, a statement that his readers had known but had forgotten. (This is one of the sad consequences of getting "dull" toward the Word; see Heb. 5:11–12.) This quotation (Heb. 12:5–6) is an "exhortation," which literally means "encouragement." Because they forgot the Word, they lost their encouragement and were ready to give up!

The key words in this quotation are "son," "children," and "sons." These words are used six times in Hebrews 12:5–8. They refer to *adult sons* and not little children. (The word "children" in Heb. 12:5 should be "sons.") A parent who would repeatedly chasten an *infant* child would be considered a monster. God deals with us as *adult* sons because we have been adopted and given an adult standing in His family (see Rom. 8:14–18; Gal. 4:1–7). The fact that the Father chastens us is proof that we are maturing, and it is the means by which we can mature even more.

Chastening is the evidence of the Father's love. Satan wants us to believe that the difficulties of life are proof that God does *not* love us, but just the opposite is true. Sometimes God's chastening is seen in His *rebukes* from the Word or from circumstances. At other times He shows His love by *punishing* ("the Lord … scourgeth") us with some physical suffering. Whatever the experience, we can be sure that His chastening hand is controlled by His loving heart. The Father does not want us to be pampered babies; He wants us to become mature adult sons and daughters who can be trusted with the responsibilities of life.

(2) Personal experience (vv. 7–11). All of us had a father and, if this father was faithful, he had to discipline us. If a child is left to himself, he grows up to become a selfish tyrant. The point the writer makes

(Heb. 12:7–8) is that a father chastens *only his own sons,* and this is proof that they *are* his children. We may feel like spanking the neighbors' children (and our neighbors may feel like spanking ours), but we cannot do it. God's chastening is proof that we are indeed His children!

I have met in my ministry people who professed to be saved, but for some reason they never experienced any chastening. If they disobeyed, they seemed to get away with it. If I resisted God's will and did not experience His loving chastening, I would be afraid that I was not saved! All true children of God receive His chastening. All others who claim to be saved, but who escape chastening, are nothing but counterfeits—illegitimate children.

Why do good earthly fathers correct their kids? So that their offspring might show them reverence (respect) and obey what they command. This is why the heavenly Father corrects us: He wants us to revere Him and obey His will. A child who does not learn subjection to authority will never become a useful, mature adult. Any of God's children who rebel against His authority are in danger of death! "Shall we not much rather be in subjection unto the Father of spirits, and live?" (Heb. 12:9). The suggestion is that, if we do not submit, *we might not live.* "There is a sin unto death" (1 John 5:16).

We can see now how this twelfth chapter relates to the five exhortations in Hebrews. As a Christian drifts from the Word and backslides, the Father chastens him to bring him back to the place of submission and obedience. (If God does not chasten, that person is not truly born again.) If a believer *persists* in resisting God's will, God may permit his life to be taken. Rather than allow His child to ruin his life further and disgrace the Father's name, God might permit him to die. God killed thousands of rebellious Jews in the wilderness (1 Cor. 10:1–12). Why should He spare us? Certainly this kind of chastening is not His usual approach, but it is possible, and we had better show Him reverence and fear. He chastens us for our profit so that we might share His holy character.

(3) The blessed results (vv. 11–13). No chastening at the time is pleasant, neither to the father nor to his son, but the benefits are profitable. I am sure that few children believe it when their parents say, "This hurts me more than it hurts you." But it is true just the same. The Father does not enjoy having to discipline His children, but the benefits afterward make the chastening an evidence of His love.

What are some of the benefits? Instead of continuing to sin, the child strives to do what is right. There is also peace instead of war—"the peaceable fruit of righteousness." The rebellion has ceased and the child is in a loving fellowship with the Father. Chastening also encourages a child to *exercise* in spiritual matters—the Word of God, prayer, meditation, witnessing, and so forth. All of this leads to a new *joy*. Paul described it: "righteousness, and peace, and joy in the Holy Ghost" (Rom. 14:17).

Of course, the important thing is how God's child responds to chastening. He can despise it or faint under it (Heb. 12:5), both of which are wrong. He should show reverence to the Father by submitting to His will (Heb. 12:9), using the experience to exercise himself spiritually (Heb. 12:11; 1 Tim. 4:7–8). Hebrews 12:12–13 sounds like a coach's orders to his team! Lift up your hands! Strengthen those knees (Isa. 35:3)! Get those lazy feet on the track (Prov. 4:26)! On your mark, get set, GO!

The example of God's Son, and the assurance of God's love, certainly should encourage us to endure in the difficult Christian race. But there is a third resource.

3. THE ENABLEMENT OF GOD'S GRACE (12:14–29)

As we run the Christian race, what is our goal? The writer explains the goal in Hebrews 12:14: *peace* with all men, and *holiness* before the Lord.

(Remember "the *peaceable* fruit of *righteousness,*" Heb. 12:11.) These two goals remind us of our Lord's high priestly ministry—King of *peace* and King of *righteousness* (Heb. 7:1–2). It requires diligence to run the race successfully lest we "fail of the grace of God" (Heb. 12:15). God's grace does not fail, but we can fail to take advantage of His grace. At the end of the chapter, there is another emphasis on grace (Heb. 12:28).

In this section, the writer encourages his readers to depend on the grace of God by urging them to look by faith in three directions.

(1) Look back—the bad example of Esau (vv. 15–17). Esau certainly failed to act on God's grace. The account is given in Genesis 25:27–34; 27:30–45. Esau was "a profane person," which means "a common person, one who lives for the world and not God." (Our English word literally means "outside the temple," or not belonging to God.) Esau despised his birthright and sold it to Jacob, and he missed the blessing because it was given to Jacob. (It was supposed to go to Jacob anyway, but it was wrong for Jacob to use trickery to get it. See Gen. 25:19–26.) Afterward, Esau tried to get Isaac to change his mind, but it was too late. Even Esau's tears availed nothing.

What sins will rob us of the enabling of God's grace? These verses tell us: lack of spiritual diligence, bitterness against others (see Deut. 29:18), sexual immorality, and living for the world and the flesh. Some people have the idea that a "profane person" is blasphemous and filthy, but Esau was a congenial fellow, a good hunter, and a man who loved his father. He would have made a fine neighbor—but he was not interested in the things of God.

God's grace does not fail, but we can fail to depend on God's grace. Esau is a warning to us not to live for lesser things.

(2) Look up—the glory of the heavenly city (vv. 18–24). The writer of Hebrews contrasted Mount Sinai and the giving of the law with the heavenly Mount Zion and the blessings of grace in the church (see Ex. 19:10–25; 20:18–21; Deut. 4:10–24). He described the solemnity and even the terror that were involved in the giving of the law (Heb. 12:18–21). The people were afraid to hear God's voice, and even Moses feared and trembled! God set boundaries around the mount, and even if an animal trespassed, it was slain with a spear ("dart"). Of course, God had to impress on His people the seriousness of His law, just as we must with our own children. This was the infancy of the nation, and children can understand reward and punishment.

What a relief it is to move from Mount Sinai to Mount Zion! Mount Sinai represents the old covenant of law, and Mount Zion represents the new covenant of grace in Jesus Christ (see Gal. 4:19–31). The heavenly city is God's Mount Zion (see Ps. 2; 110:1–2, 4). This is the city that the patriarchs were looking for by faith (Heb. 11:10, 14–17). The earthly Jerusalem was about to be destroyed by the Romans, but the heavenly Jerusalem would endure forever.

He described the citizens that make up the population of this city. Innumerable angels are there. The church is there, for believers have their citizenship in heaven (Phil. 3:20 NIV), and their names are written in heaven (Luke 10:20). "Firstborn" is a title of dignity and rank. Esau was actually Isaac's firstborn, but he rejected his privileges and lost his blessing and birthright.

God is there, of course, and so are the Old Testament saints ("spirits of just men made perfect"). Jesus Christ the Mediator is there, the One who shed His blood for us. We learned that Abel is still speaking (Heb. 11:4), and here we discover that Christ's blood speaks "better things than that of Abel" (Heb. 12:24). Abel's blood spoke from the earth and cried for justice (Gen. 4:10), while Christ's blood speaks from heaven and announces mercy for sinners. Abel's blood made Cain feel guilty (and rightly so) and drove him away in despair (Gen. 4:13–15), but Christ's blood frees us from guilt and has opened the way into the presence of God. Were it not for the blood of the new covenant, we could not enter this heavenly city!

"Why is there so little preaching and teaching about heaven?" a friend asked me. And then he gave his own answer, which is probably correct. "I guess we have it so good on earth, we just don't think about heaven."

When the days are difficult and we are having a hard time enduring, that is when we should look up and contemplate the glories of heaven. Moses "endured, as seeing him who is invisible" (Heb. 11:27). The patriarchs endured as they looked ahead to the city God was preparing for them. One way to lay hold of God's grace is to look ahead by faith to the wonderful future He has prepared for us.

(3) Look ahead—the unshakable kingdom (vv. 25–29). God is speaking to us today through His Word and His providential workings in the world. We had better listen! If God shook things at Sinai and those who refused to hear were judged, how much more responsible are we today who have experienced the blessings of the new covenant! God today is shaking things. (Have you read the newspapers lately?) He wants to tear down the "scaffolding" and reveal the unshakable realities that are eternal. Alas, too many people (including Christians) are building their lives on things that can shake.

The "shaking" quotation is from Haggai 2:6 and refers to that time when the Lord shall return and fill His house with glory. As events draw nearer to that time, we shall see more shaking in this world. But a Christian can be confident, for he shall receive an unshakable kingdom. In fact, he is a part of God's kingdom today.

What shall we do as we live in a shaking world? Listen to God speak and obey Him. Receive grace day by day to serve Him "with reverence and godly fear." Do not be distracted or frightened by the tremendous changes going on around you. Keep running the race with endurance. Keep looking to Jesus Christ. Remember that your Father loves you. And draw on God's enabling grace.

While others are being frightened, you can be confident!

QUESTIONS FOR PERSONAL REFLECTION
OR GROUP DISCUSSION

1. In what ways is your spiritual life like a race?

2. Who are the people you look up to as having run the race the way you hope to run it?

3. List the kinds of things that weigh you down in your spiritual journey.

4. What keeps us from letting go of the things that weigh us down?

5. What specifics from Jesus' life help you know how to travel on your spiritual journey?

6. Runners in a race look toward the finish line and any prize (material or otherwise) that will come from their finishing the race. What do we look forward to in finishing this race that we call the Christian life?

7. List some ways in which we can be chastened by God.

8. Give some examples from your own life of the difference between looking ahead to a future hope and looking behind?

9. How does God's grace make a difference in the race you run?

10. How can we help each other to look ahead and finish the race?

Chapter Twelve

PARDON ME, YOUR FAITH IS SHOWING

(Hebrews 13)

As you read this last chapter in Hebrews, you get the impression that the writer had a great deal of miscellaneous matter to discuss and saved it till the end. In Hebrews 12, we were rejoicing on Mount Zion, and now we are discussing such everyday topics as hospitality, marriage, church officers, and who was the last one to be released from jail.

But in the Bible, there is no division between doctrine and duty, revelation and responsibility. The two always go together. The emphasis in this last section of the book is on *living by faith*. The writer presented the great *examples* of faith in Hebrews 11, and the *encouragements* to faith in Hebrews 12. In Hebrews 13, he presents the *evidences* of faith that should appear in our lives if we are really walking by faith and not by sight. There are four such evidences.

1. ENJOYING SPIRITUAL FELLOWSHIP (13:1–6)

The *basis* for this fellowship is brotherly love. As Christians, these Hebrew people no doubt had been rejected by their friends and families. But the deepest kind of fellowship is not based on race or family relationship; it is based on the spiritual life we have in Christ. A church fellowship based on anything other than love for Christ and for one another simply will not last. (For other references to "brotherly love" see Romans 12:10; 1 Thessalonians 4:9–10; 1 Peter 1:22; and 2 Peter 1:7.)

Where there is true Christian love, there will also be *hospitality* (Heb. 13:2). This was an important ministry in the early church because persecution drove many believers away from their homes. Also, there were traveling ministers who needed places to stay (3 John 5–8). Many poor saints could not afford to stay in an inn, and since the churches met in homes (Rom. 16:5), it was natural for a visitor to just stay with his host. Pastors are supposed to be lovers of hospitality (Titus 1:8), but all saints should be "given to hospitality" (Rom. 12:13).

Moses (Gen. 18) gave the story of Abraham showing generous hospitality to Jesus Christ and two of His angels. Abraham did not know who they were when he welcomed them; it was only later that he discovered the identities of his illustrious guests. You and I may not entertain angels in a literal sense (though it is possible), but *any* stranger could turn out to be a messenger of blessing to us. (The word *angel* simply means "messenger.") Often we have had guests in our home who have turned out to be messengers of God's blessings.

Love also expresses itself in *concern* (Heb. 13:3). It was not unusual for Christians to be arrested and imprisoned for their faith. To identify with these prisoners might be dangerous, yet Christ's love demanded a ministry to them. To minister to a Christian prisoner in the name of Christ is to minister to Christ Himself (Matt. 25:36, 40). In our free country we are not arrested for our religious beliefs, but in other parts of the world, believers suffer for their faith. How we need to pray for them and share with them as the Lord enables us!

The home is the first place where Christian love should be practiced

(Heb. 13:4). A Christian home begins with a Christian marriage in the will of God. This means loyalty and purity. Sex outside of marriage is sinful and destructive. Sex within the protective bonds of marriage can be enriching and glorifying to God. Fornication is committed by unmarried persons and adultery by married persons. (However, in the New Testament, the term "fornication" can refer to many kinds of sexual sins. See Acts 15:20 and 1 Cor. 6:18.)

How does God judge fornicators and adulterers? Sometimes they are judged in their own bodies (Rom. 1:24–27). Certainly they will be judged at the final judgment (Rev. 21:8; 22:15). Believers who commit these sins certainly may be forgiven, but they will lose rewards in heaven (Eph. 5:5ff.). David was forgiven, but he suffered the consequences of his adultery for years to come, and he suffered in the hardest way: through his own children.

In these days, when sexual sins are paraded as entertainment in movies and on television, the church needs to take a stand for the purity of the marriage bond. A dedicated Christian home is the nearest thing to heaven on earth, and it starts with a Christian marriage.

If we love God and others as we should, then we will have a right relationship to *material things* (Heb. 13:5–6). Times of suffering can either be times of selfishness or times of service. It is not easy to take "joyfully the spoiling of your goods" (Heb. 10:34). But with the economic and ecological problems in our world today, comfortable Christians may soon find themselves doing without some luxuries that they now consider necessities.

A Christian couple was ministering to believers in Eastern Europe, behind the former Iron Curtain. The couple had brought in Christian literature, blankets, and other necessary items. At the church gathering, the couple assured the believers that Christians in America were praying for believers in Eastern Europe.

"We are happy for that," one believer replied, "but we feel that Christians in America need more prayer than we do. We here in Eastern Europe are suffering, but you in America are very comfortable; and it is always harder to be a good Christian when you are comfortable."

The word *covetousness* literally means "love of money"; but it can be applied to a love for *more* of anything. Someone asked millionaire Bernard Baruch, "How much money does it take for a rich man to be satisfied?" Baruch replied, "Just a million more than he has." Covetousness is the desire for more, whether we need it or not.

Contentment cannot come from material things, for they can never satisfy the heart. Only God can do that. "Watch out! Be on your guard against all kinds of greed; a man's life does not consist in the abundance of his possessions" (Luke 12:15 NIV). When we have God, we have all that we need. The material things of life can decay or be stolen, but *God* will never leave us or forsake us. This promise was made to Joshua when he succeeded Moses (Deut. 31:7–8; Josh. 1:5, 9), and it is fulfilled to us in Jesus Christ (Matt. 28:20; Acts 18:9–10).

The affirmation of faith in Hebrews 13:6 comes from Psalm 118:6. This is a messianic psalm and is fulfilled in Jesus Christ, so we may claim this promise for ourselves. It was a source of great peace to the early Christians to know that they were safe from the fear of man, for no man could do anything to them apart from God's will. Men might take their goods, but God would meet their needs.

A woman said to evangelist D. L. Moody, "I have found a promise that helps me when I am afraid. It is Psalm 56:3—'What time I am afraid, I will trust in thee.'"

Mr. Moody replied, "I have a better promise than that! Isaiah 12:2—'I will trust, and not be afraid.'"

Both promises are true and each has its own application. The important thing is that we know Jesus Christ as our Lord and Helper, and that we not put our trust in material things. Contented Christians are people with priorities, and material things are not high on their priority lists.

2. SUBMITTING TO SPIRITUAL LEADERSHIP (13:7–9, 17, 24)

Three times the writer used the designation "Them that have the rule over you." The phrase refers to the spiritual leaders of the local assemblies. The church is an organism, but it is also an organization. If an organism is not organized, it will die! Wherever Paul went, he founded local churches and ordained qualified believers to lead them (Acts 14:23; Titus 1:5). "Saints ... bishops [elders] and deacons" (Phil. 1:1) summarize the membership and leadership of the New Testament churches.

Each Christian has three responsibilities toward the spiritual leaders in his local church.

(1) Remember them (vv. 7–9). The word *remember* may suggest that these leaders were dead, perhaps martyred, and should not be forgotten. How easy it is to forget the courageous Christians of the past whose labors and sacrifices make it possible for us to minister today. But while we do not worship people or give them the glory, it is certainly right to honor them for their faithful work (1 Thess. 5:12–13).

These leaders probably had led the readers to Christ because the leaders had spoken the Word to them. When you recall that few Christians then had copies of the Scriptures, you can see the importance of this personal ministry of the Word. Today, we can read the Bible for ourselves, listen to radio or television sermons, and even listen to our computers. We are in danger of taking the Word for granted.

The believers could no longer hear their departed leaders speak, but they could imitate their faith and consider its outcome, or "end." This could refer to their deaths, suggesting that some of them were martyred. However, I believe that "the outcome of their way of life" (Heb. 13:7 NIV) is given in

Hebrews 13:8: "Jesus Christ, the same yesterday, and today, and forever." Their lives pointed to Christ! Church leaders may come and go, but Jesus Christ remains the same, and it is Christ who is the center of our faith.

After I had announced my resignation from a church I had been pastoring for several years, one of the members said to me, "I don't see how I'm going to make it without you! I depend so much on you for my spiritual help!"

My reply shocked him. "Then the sooner I leave, the sooner you can start depending on the Lord. Never build your life on any servant of God. Build your life on Jesus Christ. He never changes."

Of course, there is always the danger of being "carried about with divers [various] and strange doctrines" (Heb. 13:9). The purpose of spiritual ministry is to establish God's people in grace, so they will not be blown around by dangerous doctrines (Eph. 4:11–14). Some recipients of the letter to the Hebrews were considering going back to Jewish laws that governed foods. The writer warned them that these dietary regulations would not profit them spiritually because they never profited the Jews spiritually! The dietary laws impressed people as being spiritual, but they were only shadows of the reality that we have in Christ (read Col. 2:16–23 carefully).

When local churches change pastors, there is a tendency also to change doctrines or doctrinal emphases. We must be careful not to go beyond the Word of God. We must also be careful not to change the spiritual foundation of the church. It is unfortunate that there is not more doctrinal preaching today, because Bible doctrine is the source of strength and growth in the church.

(2) Obey them (v. 17). When a servant of God is in the will of God, teaching the Word of God, the people of God should submit and obey. This does not mean that pastors should be dictators. "Neither [be] lords over God's heritage" (1 Peter 5:3). Some church members have a flippant attitude toward pastoral authority, and this is dangerous. One day every pastor will have to give an account of his ministry to the Lord, and he wants to be able to do it with joy. A disobedient Christian will find on that day that the results of disobedience are unprofitable, not for the pastor, but for himself.

Quite frankly, it is much easier to win souls than it is to "watch for souls" (see Ezek. 3:16–21). The larger a church grows, the more difficult it becomes to care for the sheep. Sad to say, there are some ministers whose only work is to preach and "run the program"; they have no desire to minister to the souls placed in their care. Some are even "hirelings" who work only for money, and who run away when danger is near (John 10:11–14). However, when a shepherd is faithful to watch for souls, it is important that the sheep obey him.

(3) Greet them (v. 24). The Jews used to greet each other with "Shalom—peace!" The Greeks often greeted one another with "Grace!" Paul combined these two and greeted the saints with, "Grace and peace be unto you!" (See 1 Cor. 1:3; 2 Cor. 1:2; and all his epistles except 1 and 2 Timothy and Titus. When Paul wrote to pastors, he greeted them with, "Grace, *mercy,* and peace." I wonder why?)

Of course, the writer of the Hebrews epistle was sending his personal greetings to the leaders of the church, but this is a good example for all of us to follow. *Every Christian should be on speaking terms with his pastor.* Never allow any "root of bitterness" to grow up in your heart (Heb. 12:15) because it will only poison you and hurt the whole church.

While it is true that each member of a local body has an important ministry to perform, it is also true that God has ordained spiritual leaders in the church. I have been privileged to preach in many churches in America, and I have noticed that where the people permit the pastors (elders) to lead, there is usually blessing and growth. I am not talking about highhanded, egotistical dictatorship, but true spiritual leadership. This is God's pattern for the church.

3. SHARING IN SPIRITUAL WORSHIP (13:10–16, 18–19)

While it is true that a new covenant Christian is not involved in the ceremonies and furnishings of an earthly tabernacle or temple, it is not true that he is deprived of the blessings that they typify. A Jew under the old covenant could point to the temple, but a Christian has a heavenly sanctuary that can never be destroyed. The Jews were proud of the city of Jerusalem, but a Christian has an eternal city, the New Jerusalem. For each of an Old Testament believer's temporary earthly items, a new covenant believer has a heavenly and eternal counterpart.

"We have an altar" (Heb. 13:10) does not suggest a material altar on earth, for that would contradict the whole message of the epistle. In the Old Testament sanctuary, the brazen altar was the place for offering blood sacrifices, and the golden altar before the veil was the place for burning incense, a picture of prayer ascending to God (Ps. 141:2). A new covenant Christian's altar is Jesus Christ, for it is *through Him* that we offer our "spiritual sacrifices" to God (Heb. 13:15; 1 Peter 2:5). We may set aside places in our church buildings and call them altars, but they are really not altars in the biblical sense. Why? Because Christ's sacrifice has already been made, once and for all, and the gifts that we bring to God are acceptable, not because of any earthly altar, but because of a heavenly altar, Jesus Christ.

The emphasis in this section is on separation from dead religion and identification with the Lord Jesus Christ in His reproach. The image comes from the Day of Atonement. The sin offering was taken outside the camp and burned completely (Lev. 16:27). Jesus Christ, our perfect sin offering, suffered and died "outside the gate" of Jerusalem. All true Christians must go out to Him, spiritually speaking, to the place of reproach and rejection.

"Why stay in Jerusalem when it is not your city?" asks the writer. "Why identify with the old covenant law when it has been done away with in Christ?"

The readers of this epistle were looking for a way to continue as Christians while escaping the persecution that would come from unbelieving Jews. "It cannot be done," the writer states in so many words. "Jerusalem is doomed. Get out of the Jewish religious system and identify with the Savior who died for you." There can be no room for compromise.

The writer names two of the "spiritual sacrifices" that we offer as Christians (Heb. 13:15–16). Note that the word *spiritual* is not in contrast to *material*, because material gifts can be accepted as spiritual sacrifices (see Phil. 4:10–20). The word *spiritual* means "spiritual in character, to be used by the Spirit for spiritual purposes." A believer's body, presented to God, is a spiritual sacrifice (see Rom. 12:1–2 NASB).

The first spiritual sacrifice is *continual praise to God* (Heb. 13:15). The words of praise from our lips, coming from our hearts, are like beautiful fruit laid on the altar. How easy it is for suffering saints to complain, but how important it is for them to give thanks to God.

The second spiritual sacrifice is *good works of sharing* (Heb. 13:16 NIV). This would certainly include the hospitality mentioned in Hebrews 13:2, as well as the ministry to prisoners in Hebrews 13:3. "Doing good" can cover a multitude of ministries: sharing food with the needy; transporting people to and from church or other places; sharing money; perhaps just being a helpful neighbor. I once had the privilege of seeing a man come to Christ because I helped him mow his lawn after his own mower broke.

Next the writer emphasizes the importance of *prayer* (Heb. 13:18–19). He was unable to visit the readers personally, but he did want their prayer help. It is possible that some of his enemies had lied about him, so he affirms his honesty and integrity. We do not know for certain who the writer was. Many think it was Paul. The reference to Timothy in Hebrews 13:23 would suggest Paul, as would also the "benediction of grace" in Hebrews 13:25 (see 2 Thess. 3:17–18). Some scholars have suggested that Peter referred to Paul's authorship of Hebrews (2 Peter 3:15–16), but that statement could also be applied to things Paul wrote in Romans. We do not know the name of the human writer of this book, nor is it important that we do.

4. EXPERIENCING SPIRITUAL LORDSHIP (13:20–21)

This benediction seems to gather together the major themes of Hebrews: peace, the resurrected Christ, the blood, the covenant, spiritual perfection (maturity), God's work in the believer. As the Good Shepherd, Jesus Christ *died* for the sheep (John 10:11). As the Great Shepherd, He *lives* for the sheep in heaven today, working on their behalf. As the Chief Shepherd, He will *come for the sheep* at His return (1 Peter 5:4). Our Shepherd cares for His own in the past, present, and future. He is the same yesterday, today, and forever!

Our Great High Priest is also our Great Shepherd. When He was on earth, He worked *for* us when He completed the great work of redemption (John 17:4). Now that He is in heaven, He is working *in us* to mature us in His will and bring us to a place of spiritual perfection. We will never reach that place until He returns (1 John 2:28—3:3), but while we are waiting, we are told to continue to grow.

The phrase "make you perfect" (Heb. 13:21) is the translation of one Greek word, *katartidzo*. This is an unfamiliar word to us, but it was familiar to the people who received this letter. The doctors knew it because it meant "to set a broken bone." To fishermen it meant "to mend a broken net" (see Matt. 4:21). To sailors it meant "to outfit a ship for a voyage." To soldiers it meant "to equip an army for battle."

Our Savior in heaven wants to equip us for life on earth. Tenderly, He wants to set the "broken bones" in our lives so that we might walk straight and run our life-races successfully. He wants to repair the breaks in the nets so that we might catch fish and win souls. He wants to equip us for battle and outfit us so that we will not be battered in the storms of life. In brief, He wants to mature us so that He can work *in* us and *through* us that which pleases Him and accomplishes His will.

How does He equip us? By tracing this word *katartidzo* in the New Testament, we can discover the tools that God uses to mature and equip His children. He uses the Word of God (2 Tim. 3:16–17) and prayer (1 Thess. 3:10) in the fellowship of the local church (Eph. 4:11–12). He also uses individual believers to equip us and mend us (Gal. 6:1). Finally, He uses suffering to perfect His children (1 Peter 5:10), and this relates to what we learned from Hebrews 12 about chastening.

What a difference it would make in our lives if we would turn Hebrews 13:20–21 into a personal prayer each day. "Lord, make me perfect in every good work to do thy will. Work in me that which is well-pleasing in thy sight. Do it through Jesus Christ and may he receive the glory."

The basis for this marvelous work is "the blood of the everlasting covenant" (Heb. 13:20). This is the new covenant that was discussed in Hebrews 8, a covenant based on the sacrifice discussed in Hebrews 10. Because this new covenant was a part of God's eternal plan of salvation, and because it guarantees everlasting life, it is called "the everlasting covenant." But apart from the death of Jesus Christ, we can share in none of the blessings named in this profound benediction.

The "Amen" at the end of the benediction closed the body of the epistle. All that remained was for the writer to add a few words of greeting and personal information.

He had written a long letter, and in it he had dealt with some profound and difficult doctrines; so he encouraged his readers to "[bear with] suffer" this letter of encouragement. This seems like a long letter to us, but he felt it was just a "few words." No doubt some members of the congregation responded negatively to this letter, while others received it and acted on it. Paul (1 Thess. 2:13) told us how we should respond to God's Word. Read the verse carefully—and practice it.

What Timothy's relationship to the group was, we do not know. He was a prominent minister in that day, and most of the Christians would either know him or know about him. These personal touches remind us that God is interested in individuals and not just in groups of people.

"They of Italy salute you" (Heb. 13:24) could mean that the writer was in Italy at the time, or that saints from Italy were with him and wanted to send their greetings.

These personal references at the end of the letter raise questions that we cannot answer now. But the total impact of Hebrews answers the important question, "How can I stand firm in a world that is shaking all around me?" The answer: know the superior person, Jesus Christ; trust His superior priesthood; and live by the superior principle of faith. Build your life on the things of heaven that will never shake.

Be confident! Jesus Christ saves to the uttermost!

QUESTIONS FOR PERSONAL REFLECTION
OR GROUP DISCUSSION

1. How is hospitality still important in our churches today as it was in the early church? What hospitality can you offer?

2. List some ways that you see the dangers of comfortable Christianity around you.

3. In what ways can we honor our spiritual leaders today even if we don't always agree with them?

4. How do you strike the balance of learning from your spiritual leaders but not depending on them for your ultimate guidance?

5. Do you need to pull away from the current religious system around you in order to live according to God's call? Or do you need to invest more in a religious institution? What makes you say that?

6. What stands in the way of our offering God a sacrifice of praise?

7. Describe how our acts of sharing affect our evangelism.

8. How does God bring us to spiritual maturity?

9. How do we join with God in an everlasting covenant?

10. How does your faith help you to stand firm in a very shaky world?

The "BE" series . . .

For years pastors and lay leaders have embraced Warren W. Wiersbe's very accessible commentary of the Bible through the individual "BE" series. Through the work of David C. Cook Global Mission, the "BE" series is part of a library of books made available to indigenous Christian workers. These are men and women who are called by God to grow the kingdom through their work with the local church worldwide. Here are a few of their remarks as to how Dr. Wiersbe's writings have benefited their ministry.

"Most Christian books I see are priced too high for me . . .
I received a collection that included 12 Wiersbe
commentaries a few months ago and I have
read every one of them.
I use them for my personal devotions every day and they
are incredibly helpful for preparing sermons.
The contribution David C. Cook is making to the
church in India is amazing."
—Pastor E. M. Abraham, Hyderabad, India

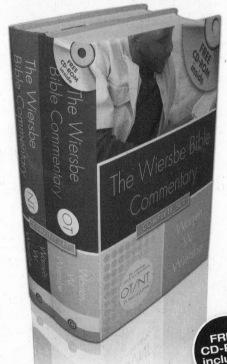